Stress Management

FOR BUSY PEOPLE

D1468382

OTHER BUSY PEOPLE BOOKS

Personal Finance for Busy People
Robert Cooke

Taxes for Busy People
Robert Cooke

Time Management for Busy People
Robert Roesch

Windows 95 for Busy People
Christian Crumlish

Word 97 for Busy People
Christian Crumlish

Windows 95 for Busy People
Ron Mansfield

Office 97 for Busy People
Steve Nelson

Quicken 98 for Busy People
Peter Weverka

Stress Management

FOR BUSY PEOPLE

Carol A. Turkington

Foreword by Dr. David Barlow

McGraw-Hill

New York   San Francisco   Washington D.C.   Auckland   Bogotá
Caracas   Lisbon   London   Madrid   Mexico City   Milan
Montreal   New Delhi   San Juan   Singapore
Sydney   Tokyo   Toronto

For Wanda

Library of Congress Catalog Card Number: 97-75821

McGraw-Hill

A Division of The McGraw·Hill Companies

Copyright © 1998 by Carol A. Turkington. All rights reserved.
Printed in the United States of America. Except as permitted under
the United States Copyright Act of 1976, no part of this publication
may be reproduced or distributed in any form or by any means, or
stored in a database or retrieval system, without the prior written
permission of the publisher.

1 2 3 4 5 6 7 8 9 0 DOC/DOC 9 0 2 1 0 9 8 7

ISBN 0-07-065535-9 (pbk.)

*The sponsoring editor for this book was Susan Barry, the assistant editor
was Griffin Hansbury, the editing supervisor was Christine Furry, and
the production supervisor was Tina Cameron. It was set in Adobe
Garamond by North Market Street Graphics.*

Printed and bound by R. R. Donnelley & Sons.

McGraw-Hill books are available at special quantity discounts to use
as premiums and sales promotions, or for use in corporate training
sessions. For more information, please write to the Director of Special
Sales, McGraw-Hill, 11 West 19th Street, New York, NY 10011. Or
contact your local bookstore.

CONTENTS

4 Attacking Stressful Thoughts and Behavior 41

FOREWORD

In the next millenium it is very likely that the number-one threat to health and well-being will not be cancer or heart disease but, rather, stress. This is because levels of stress are ever on the increase in our society; and we are recognizing that the effects of chronic stress are broad and deep. For example, we have learned that stress, and the closely related emotional reactions of anxiety and depression, make it more likely that we will catch a cold and suffer worse with a cold than if we weren't under stress. We are more likely to die, or will die more quickly, from several varieties of cancer if we are stressed or depressed than if we are not. And, in a relatively new discovery, parts of our brain that contribute to emotional and cognitive functioning, such as memory, are likely to be permanently damaged if we are chronically stressed.

For all of these reasons it is imperative that we make stress control a priority in our busy lives, right up there with ensuring the financial and material well-being of ourselves and our families. For, if our health and mental functioning deteriorates sufficiently under chronic and unrelenting stress, we won't be able to enjoy the benefits of our labors or the rich and rewarding nature of our closest relationships.

At the Center for Anxiety and Related Disorders at Boston University we study stress, anxiety, and related problems on a daily basis as we attempt to develop new and more effective interventions for these stubborn disorders. We know that stress and anxiety in severe forms can not only kill you, by making you more susceptible to life-threatening diseases, but can also incapacitate you in your day-to-day living. We see clients all the time who have let their problems go to the point where they are either no longer able to function or can function only with great difficulty. We also know that we can reduce stress and anxiety and their disorders substantially with proven and effective, brief psychological interventions in which individuals actually learn new principles and procedures that help them change the pace of their lives. Furthermore, these changes seem to be "permanent" in that, once learned, the person who benefits from these procedures finds the rewards so satisfying as to make these new coping styles a natural part of their day-to-day life.

But we also know that most people are too busy to stop and take advantage of these procedures or they are not aware that programs such as this are available. Now, in this "busy people" series, Carol Turkington has distilled the latest findings on reducing stress into an easy-to-read manual that will benefit everyone who takes a few minutes to digest the wisdom embodied within this brief guide. Turkington, with long years of experience in translating cutting-edge findings from psychological science into usable and useful information for the population at large, has done an excellent job in making this stress-reduction program among the most user-friendly I have ever encountered. Those who suffer from the effects of stress, and that is most of us, should carry this book with them and take a few minutes each day to incorporate the important, helpful, and beneficial principles that are found on its pages.

David H. Barlow Ph.D., Director

Center for Stress and Anxiety-Related Disorders
at Boston University
and Professor of Psychology, Boston University

INTRODUCTION

Your alarm clock didn't go off. Your only clean suit is lying in a heap on the closet floor. At the breakfast table, your daughter tells you she needs baking soda for her volcano project, and you're all out. The dog eats a Brillo pad, the cat throws up on the couch, and the dishwasher blows a gasket. Your car's out of gas, there's an unexpected detour on the way to work, and as the heavens open you remember you left your umbrella on the dining room table.

It's not even 7 A.M. and already your blood pressure is out of control. At work, you can't find an important file, your secretary gave her notice, and there's a note on your desk telling you that Mike Wallace has called about that investment scheme your brother-in-law talked you into.

Stress. That eye-popping, stomach-gripping, face-flushing intensity can pulverize your control quicker than a Mixmaster. It's everywhere, it's inescapable, and it's definitely unhealthy. But stress by itself can't hurt anyone—it's how you *respond* to stress that counts.

We know you're busy—you may not have time to wade through endless chapters covering the ins and outs of stress management. That's where this book comes in. One of a series of Busy People guides, this one will present you with news you can use—in direct, digestible bites. If you're interested in meditation to ease stress, you won't have to page through endless chapters to find it. If you simply want to cut to the chase—to learn *how* to meditate without spending time drilling yourself about *why* it works—this book's reader-friendly style will help you do just that. You can use this either as a quick reference or as a complete analysis of stress management, depending on what you're looking for.

As our civilization zooms toward the next millennium, it's going to be imperative that we learn how to deal with stress—or face serious consequences. The goal of this book is to help you meet that challenge—fast!

In less time than it takes to assemble a Lava lamp, you can zip through this book and be able to:

- Identify your stress.
- Learn to relax.
- Tap your brain's success circuits.
- Slow your heart rate.
- Ease your headaches.
- Lower your blood pressure.
- Learn a new way to breathe.
- Tame negative self-talk.
- Become more assertive.
- Cope with anxiety and anger.
- Manage your time.
- Eat your way stress-free.
- Exercise away stress.

Along the way, you'll find timesaving tips and techniques and lots of advice about how to ease your stress.

But remember, although you'll be learning about lots of different ways to beat stress, you don't need to use *all* of them—and anyway, who's got all that time? Choose the things that make sense to you and fit in with your busy lifestyle, and jettison the rest. Or save them up for that halcyon day when you've got time to explore *all* the backroads to relaxation.

A Guide to Using This Book

You can use this book as a reference, or you can read it from cover to cover. Here's a quick rundown of the important elements you'll find as you go along:

Fast Forwards

Each chapter begins with a section called Fast Forward. These sections should always be your first stop if you're an expert on stress strategies—or you're just impatient. They will offer you everything you need to know in one quick bite—sort of the *Reader's Digest* version of the chapter. Each one is a nifty little illustrated reference guide that summarizes the key points found in the chapter.

To make things easier, each one will include page references to guide you to more complete explanations later in the chapter.

Habits & Strategies

These notes convey timesaving tips that appear as reader-friendly highlighted boxes throughout the text. Even if you're already a stress-busting expert, don't overlook these timesaving tips, techniques, and tidbits. They'll give you the big picture and help you plan ahead.

Instant Stress Releasers

These brief tips will be sprinkled throughout the book as quick ways to ease stress.

Cautions

There's a right way and a wrong way to do most things in life, and with many of the stress-busting strategies, some of you could hurt yourselves if you don't follow directions. Cautions will highlight those danger areas. (For example, readers with diagnosed heart disease should not try some of the stress tests without approval from a doctor.)

Definitions

Clear, concise definitions of unfamiliar words and phrases, inserted right into the text so you'll understand what you're reading immediately.

STEP BY STEP

Step-by-Steps

Many of the tips in this book really need detailed instructions to carry out (such as the breathing exercises). You'll easily be able to recognize these step-by-step boxes where you can find these details.

Throughout the book, cross-references and other minor asides appear in margin notes like this one.

What's Next?

At the end of each chapter, you'll find a What's Next? section alerting you to what's coming up.

Let's Go!

Ready? Then grab a chair and let's dig into the tips from the best of the best stress experts before you lose one more gray hair!

Stress Management

FOR BUSY PEOPLE

1

How Stress Affects You

INCLUDES

- Stress and your body
- Keep a stress log
- Types of stress
- Chart your response to stress

FAST FORWARD

Stress and Your Body ➤ *p. 4*

The fight-or-flight response of our ancestors was important to survival in prehistoric times; today, with so little physical outlet for our tension, stress tends to cause an unhealthy buildup of hormones that can lead to significant disease. Stress produces the following effects:

- Digestion slows down.
- Breathing speeds up.
- Heart races and blood pressure soars.
- Perspiration cools the body.
- Muscles tense.
- Blood clots faster.
- Sugar and fat pour into the blood.

Stress and Disease ➤ *p. 7*

Stress causes a wide variety of disease, including:

- Allergies
- Asthma
- Migraines
- Irritable bowel syndrome
- Eczema
- Psoriasis
- Hives
- High blood pressure
- Heart disease

Stress and Your Heart ➤ *p. 8*

Unrelenting stress can cause a variety of heart problems, including:

- Plaque buildup
- Blood clots
- Thickened blood
- Heart attack
- Stroke

Stress and Immunity ➤ *p. 9*

If you're stressed, you're more likely to get sick because you can't seem to fight off infections. The more stress, the fewer antibodies you will produce. You're also more likely to be infected with viruses linked to cancer, including:

- Liver cancer
- Leukemia
- Some types of skin cancer

Stress and Your Digestion ➤ *p. 9*

Stress can boost stomach acid secretion and has been linked to:

- Esophageal spasm
- Diarrhea
- Irritable bowel syndrome
- Spastic colon

Stress and Your Frame ➤ *p. 10*

Stress hormones can eventually interfere with your bone density, resulting in significant bone disease in women.

Stress and Your Skin ➤ *p. 10*

Stress can cause profound effects on your skin. In fact, experts believe a wide range of skin problems, including acne, eczema, rosacea, herpes, psoriasis, and hives, can be worsened or even triggered by stress.

Stress can have a huge impact on every part of your body. In this chapter, we'll look at how stress can affect different parts of your body and its processes.

Stress and Your Body

Stress is here for a reason. Contrary to popular belief, it's not a condition that we made up in the 20th century. In fact, stress is powerful because it *has* been around for—well, ever since the beginning. The fact is, our stress responses can be traced to the dawn of time, when the cave dwellers who responded best to stress lived longest to tell the tale.

Our legal system now recognizes stress as a consequence of crime. Courts have ruled that a victim really can be "scared to death."

Fighting or Fleeing

There's your ancestor, peacefully smoking a reed by the fire when suddenly he sees the glowing eyes of a saber-toothed tiger at the edge of the forest. Instantly, his body goes into fight-or-flight mode, and in a matter of seconds the following occur:

- *Digestion slows down.* His blood gets shunted to muscles and brain. (If you're staring down a hairy mastodon, your body doesn't need to waste time digesting last night's wildebeest.) Today, you may experience this as butterflies in your stomach.
- *Breathing speeds up.* The cave dweller's breath would speed up to prepare him for action. Did you ever try to catch your breath after getting scared?
- *Heart races and blood pressure soars.* His blood would be forced to all parts of the body to prepare to fight or flee. Remember what it feels like when your heart pounds from fear?
- *Perspiration cools the body.* The ability to sweat under stress allows the body to burn more energy. When you're getting ready to face that hostile boardroom, do you think about using more deodorant?
- *Muscles tense.* That caveman was ready to run from danger. Today, you might feel a stiff neck or aching back after a stressful day.

One out of five people responds to stress in a destructive way.

- *Blood clots faster.* Under stress, you release chemicals to make blood clot quicker in case of injury.
- *Sugar and fats pour into the blood.* If that caveman had to slay an attacker, he had the internal fuel to do it. Have you ever been surprised by your extraordinary strength and endurance during an emergency?

Stress and Modern Man

All of these physical reactions were great for the cave dwellers, who lived life on the physiological edge. Who knew when the next woolly mammoth would come charging out of the forest intent on a meal? For our ancestors, this fight-or-flight mechanism was important to survival.

Today we've got those same unconscious body responses to stress—but we don't have any woolly mammoths to contend with, whatever we might privately think about our boss. But we *do* still have stress, and lots of it. When you're threatened, you may brace yourself, but you try to control most other reactions. Dealing with that annoying telephone solicitor might be stressful, but it's not life threatening. You can't punch the salesperson in the nose and *release* all that pent-up stress, no matter how much you'd like to. So you take all of those tiny, brief stresses and you swallow them. Psychologists call it *internalizing.*

Your body calls it destructive.

It's a good bet you don't even realize how many tiny, inconsequential, and annoying stresses you deal with and move on. Try keeping a log of just one day out of your life.

Keep a Log

Tomorrow morning, take a pad along and jot down the stress producers you encounter. I'm not talking major stress here—I mean the little stuff. Write down when . . .

Americans make 187 million visits to the doctor each year for stress-related complaints.

- You wake up late.
- The kids whine about making their beds.
- The cat jumps into the bread drawer.
- You can't find clean placemats because somebody forgot to do the wash last night.

- Your kids complain they have no clean underwear (there's that wash problem again . . .).
- You're out of juice boxes for the kids' lunch.

And so on. . . . You're not even out the door, and odds are that you've already logged quite a few minor, everyday moments of stress that usually go unremarked. If you work inside the home, just trying to get through all the thousand and one tasks in one day can represent a huge burden of stress.

No Outlet for Stress

Each time you feel a burst of stressful frustration, you probably just swallow your irritation and keep going . . . again . . . and again.

You're triggering your stress response more often—your body is being overrun with stress chemicals—and they have nowhere to go. Most situations don't provide an outlet for all that extra energy our bodies produce so well.

Let's face it, we're a people with no one to fight and nowhere to run. We struggle with heightened arousal that can't go anywhere. But because it doesn't go away, all that stress can start to harm our bodies. Stress can:

- Destroy your appetite
- Cripple your immune system
- Shut down processes that repair your tissues
- Block sleep
- Break down your bones

When you experience stress, your body pumps out hormones such as cortisol and epinephrine. These hormones are the ones that boost heart rate, blood pressure, metabolism, and physical activity.

When the stressful moment is over, the stress hormones should drop to normal. But sometimes they don't; sometimes they stay at high levels in the blood. And when one stress piles on top of another, the stress hormones may never drop below the crisis level in your blood. Continued exposure to stress often leads to mental and physical symptoms:

- Anxiety
- Depression

Too many stress hormones disrupt your ability to cope. Less than 20 percent of people are effective in crises such as fires or floods.

- Palpitations
- Muscular aches/pains

Types of Stress

By this time, you may have realized that there are different varieties of stress. There is the *mild, brief sort:*

- Missing your bus
- Losing your Phillies tickets
- Almost hitting an animal with your car

Moderate stress lasts longer and is harder to deal with:

- Preparing for a wedding
- Staying late at the office more than once
- Temporary absence of a child or partner

Then there is the *severe, chronic stress:*

- Death of a child or spouse
- Divorce

Stress and Disease

Stress doesn't always directly cause illness, but it can be a contributing factor. Among other things, stress has been linked to:

- Allergies
- Asthma
- Migraines
- Irritable bowel syndrome
- Eczema
- Psoriasis
- Hives
- High blood pressure
- Heart disease

Stress and the Heart

Irregular heartbeats (arrhythmia) peak on Mondays and Fridays. The dread of going to work and the excitement about getting away from work is too much for some folks. More than 250,000 sudden cardiac deaths each year are caused by a rapid, dramatic change in the normal heartbeat.

We've all had killer days at the office—but recent research suggests that this could be happening literally. How does it work? As stress boosts your heart's demand for oxygen, it cuts the body's supply of oxygen at the same time. Stress can even restrict blood flow to the heart and overstimulate its action.

There's no end to the nasty things stress has been found to do to the heart. For one thing, stress contributes to the buildup of plaque in your arteries. When you're standing there on the trading floor with a fistful of orders and your customers are shouting "*Sell!*" you can bet your body is pumping out harmful substances that clog up your arteries. Adrenaline is pouring into your bloodstream at the same time, leading to blood clots and thickened blood. These clots can stick to your artery walls or move along into narrower arteries or capillaries where they can trigger a heart attack or stroke.

CAUTION

It's your working blood pressure that heralds disaster, not the one your nurse gets while you're lying around in the doctor's office. This means that those doctor's readings don't represent your true blood pressure or your true risk.

Type A Personality

Also known as *hot responders,* these folks tend to be:

- Overly competitive
- Aggressive
- Compulsive
- Driven by deadlines

You can teach yourself to have high blood pressure— and you can unlearn it!

Type As overreact to the most minor stress by pumping out stress hormones—perhaps several episodes a day. Researchers think that these surging hormones in some way damage blood vessels.

Even non–type As under considerable stress run similar risks of heart problems.

Stress and Immunity

Doctors are now dealing with the effects of stress in kids. One study's findings: by the age of 6, many have already laid the groundwork for severe high blood pressure.

If you're under lots of stress, chances are you're more likely to get sick. Ever been under lots of stress and notice that suddenly you're getting cold sores, yeast infections, and colds more often? People with herpes simplex infections also find that they have lesions during periods of stress.

Your First Line of Defense

Your immune system is your body's protection against infection from viruses, bacteria, and toxins. It's weakened by stress. Its chemical substances, which help promote healing when the body is injured, are all inhibited by stress. Fear, depression, anger, and other negative emotions depress the immune system, too. Long- and short-term stress can affect its vitality. Bereavement, depression, loneliness, and chronic stress all decimate your body's natural killer cells.

Scientists have found that people who are stressed out just can't seem to marshal the forces in their immune systems to fight off infections. This is measured in how many antibodies you can produce. The more stress you have, the more difficult it is for your body to make these immune system soldiers. Experts also think that people with weak immune systems caused by high-stress hormones are much more likely to be infected with viruses linked to cancers such as:

Stress causes cholesterol to rise as much or more than does diet!

- Liver cancer
- Leukemia
- Some types of skin cancer

Stress and Digestion

Scientists know that stress can affect stomach acid secretion. Studies have suggested that a wide variety of diseases of the digestive tract are probably related to stress, including esophageal spasm, diarrhea, irritable bowel syndrome, and spastic colon.

Stress and Your Frame

When the stress hormones flood your body, they can eventually interfere with your bone density. In one study, 40-year-old women with high levels of depression and stress hormones in their blood had the equivalent of 70-year-old bones.

Stress and Your Skin

If you'd like more information about stress, turn to Appendix A to find some neat Web sites dedicated to stress and stress reduction. Although we didn't list them all here, there are plenty of other Web sites on the Internet that offer a wide variety of stress-reduction products. You can find them by following the hyperlinks on various stress-related Web sites. Happy hunting!

Stress can cause profound effects on our skin. In fact, experts believe a wide range of skin problems—acne, eczema, rosacea, herpes, psoriasis, and hives, for example—can be worsened or even triggered by stress.

You're most at risk for developing stress-related skin problems if you have problem skin to start with. When people work late, don't eat healthy meals, neglect their exercise or sleep needs, the strain shows up first in the skin.

Preventing Stress-Related Skin Damage

If you think stress is worsening the condition of your skin:

- Don't touch your face, and don't scratch or open blemishes.
- Use a moisturizer to combat dryness. Avoid exotic ingredients that could cause an allergic reaction.
- Drink more water; it will affect the skin's tone and texture.

Stress and Your Behavior

Stress can make you unhappy—filled with feelings of depression, anxiety, panic, inadequacy, pessimism, and dissatisfaction. It can make you hard to live with, since people who are stressed are often irritable, irrational, and hostile.

Stress can affect your work performance as well, causing you to be forgetful, lethargic, and unable to make decisions.

Thinking Positively

If it takes too much effort to cope with your environment, the resulting stress can impact your health.

You may be feeling depressed right now with all this talk about the negative effects of stress on our health. But it's vital to remember that while your emotions and beliefs can influence your susceptibility to disease, they can also be the conduits of healing. Stress, anger, and depression can pump out stress hormones that can be profoundly harmful. At the same time, positive beliefs, expectations, attitudes, and feelings can lead to changes in the brain that lead to healing responses.

If the mind and the body are connected, that connection doesn't lead just one way. Stress can hurt you, but positive emotions can heal.

What's Next?

Feeling more relaxed yet? Probably not—you've just been learning all the ways stress can make you sick. Sit down, put your feet up, and get ready to move on to Chapter 2. There you'll learn how to identify the sources of your stress, the many hidden faces stress can wear, and how to measure your body's response to stress.

Identifying Your Stress

INCLUDES

- Determining your lifestyle stresses

- Detecting hidden stress

- Measuring your body's responses

FAST FORWARD

Kinds of Stress ➤ *p. 15*

There are two kinds of stress: *internal* and *external* stress. Internal stress comes from inside us—our attitudes, thoughts, and feelings that make our stress worse. External stress comes from outside us, including jobs, relationships, home, money, health, and so on.

Where Is Your Stress Coming From? ➤ *p. 17*

Different people get stressed by different things. If you want to solve your stress problem, first you have to find out what parts of your life are out of control and what parts you're handling OK.

Keep a Stress Diary ➤ *p. 22*

The best way to find out what's causing you stress is to keep a stress diary.

1. Monitor your level of stress every hour.
2. Record what's causing you stress, how and when.

If It's Tuesday, I Must Be Stressed . . . ➤ *p. 22*

Sometimes it's obvious when you're feeling stress, and sometimes it's not. If you're not facing up to your harried life, the stress your body is encountering will erupt in some other way:

1. Mental
2. Physical
3. Emotional
4. Behavioral

Test Your Stress Level ➤ *p. 26*

Odds are, if you've picked up this book, you're already feeling mighty stressed—or you know someone who is. But that generalized feeling of stress—that teeth-grinding, vein-throbbing feeling of impending explosion may be just that—generalized. A lot of us are bowed down by irritations so frustrating we *feel* a sort of global tension, but we don't always understand exactly what's causing it. If you're going to learn how to handle stress, it stands to reason that first you've got to figure out where it's coming from.

When you feel stress, you need to recognize where it's coming from.

In this chapter, you'll learn about the two basic sorts of stress and where your particular stress may be coming from. You'll learn to detect a wide variety of stress triggers—and later on in the chapter, you can take some short quizzes to zoom in on your potential problem areas.

Two Kinds of Stress

Basically, there are two kinds of stress: things that come at you from the outside (what the experts call *external stressors*) and those tendencies and behaviors that originate within each of us (the *internal stressors*).

The Evil Outside

External stressors are everywhere, that everyday garden-variety *daily stress* we all experience when we can't find our keys, the traffic is gridlocked, or the washing machine breaks down. When you face lots of these daily stresses in quick succession, it can feel as if you're being nibbled to death by rabbits. Then there are the *organizational stresses*—those irritations you run into when you try to get that toxic waste dump moved into another state and you run into rules, regulations, and red tape. There are the constant *social stresses* of life as a human being, dealing with other people's tempers, aggression, and anger. Let's not forget the *major life events,* when you lose your job, don't get a promotion, have a new baby, or experience a death in the family.

These types of external stresses can keep us all perspiring and palpitating, and there's certainly plenty of that to go around. But most of our stress, oddly enough, we seem to generate ourselves. We make poor lifestyle choices, we have stressful personality traits, we're hard on ourselves, we fall into unproductive mind traps.

The Evil Within . . .
Negative Self-Talk

Many of us talk to ourselves in ways we would never address others.

- "I'm so stupid."
- "Why is he staring at me like that? What did I do?"
- "I'm not going to get excited about this new job. It's probably just as bad as all the others."

Living an Unhealthy Life

Another common way of generating your own stress is through unhealthy lifestyle choices.

- Do you drink more than two mugs of coffee a day? More than a glass of wine a day?
- Have you quit smoking yet?
- Do you try to cram 25 odd jobs into a 10-job day?
- Do you catch the last moments of *David Letterman* despite the fact that you have to get up at 6 A.M. the next day?

Mental Traps

Then there are those mental traps just waiting to ambush us just when we think we've got things all together. These are guaranteed to generate some stress:

- "Now that I've lost 25 pounds, my life will be perfect!"
- "The boss didn't smile at me this morning. He must hate my report!"

Americans make 187 million visits a year to their doctors with complaints stemming from too much stress.

- "I don't care what personnel says, I've been using an electric typewriter for the past 20 years and I'm not about to start using a computer now!"
- "My speech didn't seem to go over well. In fact, I'm probably the worst speaker in this company. I'm the worst speaker ever. I'm sure everyone was laughing at me. I'll never get any better. I shouldn't even try."

Personality Blues . . .

Some of us were just born with personality traits that seem perfectly designed to cause us stress, and lots of it. You may think that stress makes you a better worker or a harder worker, but eventually it's likely to take a toll on your body.

- Are you a hard-driving, explosive type A? Do you pound your shoes on your desk when things don't go your way?
- "It doesn't have to be right, it has to be perfect or I'm not satisfied."
- "Working 80-hour weeks at the company will pay off someday."
- Do you say yes to every request, no matter how unfair it may be to you, simply because you have a desperate need to please everybody else?

Where Is Your Stress Coming From?

Of course, it's a good idea to understand the basic types of stress. But you also need to understand where your own particular problems lie if you want to learn how to vanquish them. What are your specific stress triggers? Maybe you can sail through a hectic staff meeting with aplomb and deflect the most hectoring complaints from other staffers, but then you fall apart on the way home when traffic is backed up and your 8-year-old's ice cream cake is melting away in the back seat.

It's important to understand that what one person finds relaxing, another finds stressful—and vice versa. You might take enormous pleasure in stretching out on a Caribbean beach with a good book. A hard-driving bank president who thrives on activity might be enormously frustrated and stressed spending unproductive time lying around getting sand in her shoes when she could be making deals and *getting things done!*

From the following list of stress triggers, see if you can identify which ones set off your fight-or-flight response.

Money

It may be the root of all evil, but it's the source of a heck of a lot of stress, too. Do any of these statements ring true for you? If so, they could reveal potent sources of stress . . .

1. Do you live from paycheck to paycheck?

2. Do you put money into savings for a rainy day, only to withdraw it again in a few weeks when it starts to shower?

3. Do you ever use your answering machine to screen out bill collectors who are calling to harass you?

4. Are there nights when you can't sleep because you're thinking about how to pay bills?

5. When it comes to finances, do you and your partner have different philosophies about money that often lead to disagreements?

Illness

1. Have you been noticing some new aches and pains, but you just haven't had time to go to the doctor?

2. Do you regularly schedule checkups for doctors and dentists?

3. Do you worry about when those faulty genes you inherited are going to kick in?

4. When you feel sick, do you refuse to stay home for anything less than pneumonia?

5. Do you secretly fear that you have a serious health problem but avoid going to the doctor because you don't want to find out the truth?

Time Management

1. Do you constantly think about the growing list of things you have to do?

2. Do you often do two things at once, like typing a business letter on the computer while talking to your sister on the phone?

3. Do you feel impatient when stuck in a line at the bank?

4. If you misplaced your calendar, would you know what you have to do tomorrow?

5. Do you have more than one calendar to coordinate important dates, engagements, to-do lists, and so on?

Spouse/Partner

1. Do you argue with your partner over minor issues?

2. Do you feel that your partner is doing his or her share around the house?

3. When was the last time the two of you got away alone together?

4. Do you find yourselves arguing about the same issues, even over things that happened years ago but that never seem to get resolved?

Social Life

1. Do you have a hard time saying no to requests to volunteer, bake, chaperone, help out?

2. Are you the one responsible for replying to invitations in your family?

3. When there's a birthday, wedding, or other gift to buy, are you the one who has to purchase and wrap it and find an appropriate card?

4. If your family goes on a vacation, are you the one who researches the destination, reserves the tickets, and makes sure the dog gets to the kennel?

Children

1. Do you regularly act as the kids' chauffeur?

2. Is there more than one toddler running around in diapers at your house right now?

3. Do you ever do anything with your kids on the spur of the moment, or is everything planned out weeks in advance?

4. Do any of your kids have more than three organized activities/lessons per week, not counting school?

5. Do you have at least one teenager in the house?

Parents

1. Are your parents living within shouting distance?

2. Have you negotiated a comfortable way to share family holidays between your folks and your partner's folks?

3. Are your parents struggling with significant health problems?

4. Do you worry about who will care for your parents when they become too old to live alone?

5. Do you still simmer with resentment about the way your folks brought you up?

Family Problems

1. Are you struggling to make a blended family work?

2. Are you dealing with issues of abuse, either from your past or in the present?

3. Now that you're all adults, do you *still* believe that mom loved your brother best?

4. Do you feel angry or depressed whenever you think about your family?

Co-workers

1. Do you feel friendly and sociable toward your co-workers?

2. Do you feel comfortable delegating tasks to other people?

3. Do you have peers among your co-workers, or do you feel isolated and alone?

4. Do you feel as though you can trust your co-workers, or are you always watching your back?

Commuting

1. When someone cuts you off on the freeway, do you feel the urge to run them over?

2. Do you have to drive more than 20 minutes to work?

3. Can you take advantage of flextime at work to ease the commute?

4. Is there any chance you could carpool?

5. Do you ever find you don't have enough gas to get to work when you leave the house in the morning?

Work

1. Is it hard to get out of bed on weekday mornings?

2. Does it feel like there just isn't enough time to finish your work?

3. Do you feel you have the power to make important decisions?

4. Do you usually work more than eight hours a day?

5. Do you feel uncomfortable delegating tasks to others?

Household Problems

1. Are you happy with your place of residence?

2. If you want to hang up a new coat, do you have to move the Electrolux to find room?

3. When the rains come, do you have to run around with a bucket to catch the drips?

4. Do you have trouble finding things?

5. Does the house feel like a pit of never-ending work?

If you've answered an emphatic *yes* to some of the above questions, and especially if the yeses were concentrated in one or two specific areas, you can begin to see some of the areas where your stress is building up. If you had lots of yeses in *many* of the categories, you might want to chart in more detail just what is going on in your life.

HABITS & STRATEGIES

Do only one thing at a time instead of three or four at once.

Keep a Stress Diary

One of the best ways of pinpointing exactly what causes you stress is to keep a stress diary, often recommended by psychologists as a way to understand exactly what's causing the problem. Before you can hope to ease your stress, you need to know where it's coming from.

In this diary, you can note your stress levels and how you feel throughout the day. Pay attention to stressful events as they occur. Every hour, record the following:

- The time
- How happy am I? (scale of 1 to 10)
- How stressed am I? (scale of 1 to 10)
- Am I enjoying my work?
- How efficient am I being right now?

Whenever a stressful event occurs (it doesn't have to be during your hourly notations), write down:

Taking control of your stress means taking control of those areas and events that cause stress. Most people expect too much of themselves and try to do too much.

- What happened
- Where it happened
- How stressed am I? (scale of 1 to 10)
- How did I handle it?

After a couple of weeks, you should see patterns emerging. Look for recurring examples of stress, how it made you feel, and how you coped.

If It's Tuesday, I Must Be Stressed . . .

One of the interesting things about stress is that it can sometimes masquerade as something else entirely. If you've been under a lot of stress at work or at home, but you're resisting the thought that you're having any problems handling things, check out the following symptoms.

Mental Symptoms

- Poor memory
- Poor concentration

- Mind racing or going blank
- Confusion
- No sense of humor

Emotional Symptoms

- Anger
- Anxiety
- Depression
- Hopelessness
- Fearfulness
- Frustration
- Guilt/shame
- Irritability
- Pessimism
- Powerlessness
- Resentment
- Restlessness
- Short temper

Physical Symptoms

- Chest pains
- Fatigue
- Frequent colds
- Headache
- Heart palpitations
- Insomnia
- Muscle aches (especially neck, shoulders, and back)
- Nausea
- Sweating
- Trembling

Behavioral Symptoms

- Crying
- Drinking excessively
- Fidgeting

- Hitting
- Nervous habits (foot tapping, nail biting, hair chewing)
- Smoking
- Swearing
- Throwing things
- Yelling

HABITS & STRATEGIES

Slow down. Talk more slowly. Try to avoid interrupting others. Walk more slowly. Drive the speed limit and don't weave in and out of lanes.

Are You at Risk for Burnout?

You get burned out when the stress of dealing with a difficult job or situation becomes too much for you. It's usually found among hard-driving, highly committed people who suddenly lose interest in and motivation for what they're doing.

You're at risk for burnout if any of the following are true:

- It's hard to turn down additional commitments or responsibilities.
- You've been under intense stress and pressure for a long time.
- You have very high standards and don't delegate well.
- You've been trying to achieve too much.
- You've been giving others too much emotional support for a long time.

Symptoms of Burnout

Unlike a supernova, you don't burn out overnight. The process happens slowly, over a long period of time. You may have mental symptoms or physical problems—or both.

- Lack of control over commitments
- The erroneous idea that you're accomplishing less
- Growing tendency to think negatively
- Loss of purpose

- Flagging energy
- Detachment from relationships

CAUTION

If you are in the late stages of burnout—feeling unmotivated and disenchanted—you need help from a good mental health professional.

Avoiding Burnout

You may be a single-minded, hard-driving workaholic, but it's possible to avoid mental burnout.

- Make sure what you're doing remains fun.
- Learn to say no.
- Reevaluate your goals.
- Reduce your commitments.
- If other people drain too much of your emotional energy, step back. Involve other people in a supportive role.
- Learn stress management skills.
- Get plenty of rest and eat a healthy diet.

HABITS & STRATEGIES

If you're at risk for burnout, repeat this mantra: I have a right to pleasure and a right to relaxation.

Too Late! I've Already Burned Out!

For some of you, this book comes too late. You're already burned out. If you're so unmotivated that you just can't face another day, you need to take some time off. If you can't, try switching to another area in your organization—that may revitalize you.

Don't wear a wristwatch if it's not absolutely necessary to be at a particular place at a certain time.

However, if you have absolutely zero interest in continuing with what you're doing, it's probably best to drop the activity. A complete change of direction may be the only solution.

Chances are, you're only unmotivated and disinterested in the one area where you've burned out.

Test Your Stress Level

Most people underestimate the amount of stress they encounter in their daily lives. As a result, mental health experts have devised a test that looks at life changes to reveal not just how stressed you are, but how stressful many seemingly everyday life events can be. Based on the idea that change usually equals stress—even if it seems like fun (for example, taking a vacation)—complete the following test:

Which Events Have You Experienced?

Check all of the events that have occurred within the past year. Then total the points.

Event	Points
Death of a spouse	100
Divorce	73
Marital separation	65
Jail term	63
Death of close family member	63
Personal injury or illness	53
Marriage	50
Fired from job	47
Marital reconciliation	45
Retirement	45
Change in family member's health	44
Pregnancy	40
Sex problems	39
New family member	39

New business	*39*
Change in financial status	*38*
Death of a close friend	*37*
Different line of work	*36*
More arguments with spouse	*35*
Mortgage or loan for major purchase	*31*
Foreclosure	*30*
Change in job responsibility	*29*
Son or daughter leaves home	*29*
In-law trouble	*29*
Outstanding personal achievement	*28*
Spouse stops or starts work	*26*
Begin or end school	*26*
Change in living conditions	*25*
Trouble with boss	*23*
Change in work hours or conditions	*20*
Change in residence	*20*
Change in schools	*20*
Change in recreation	*19*
Change in church activities	*19*
Mortgage or loan for smaller purchase (car, etc.)	*17*
Change in sleeping habits	*16*
Change in number of family get-togethers	*15*
Change in eating habits	*15*
Vacation	*13*
Holidays	*12*
Minor violations of law	*11*

More than 300
Your stress level is high. You need some stress intervention techniques now!

150–300
Borderline high stress. You need to reduce the number of high-impact changes, if possible.

0–150
Your stress level based on life changes at the moment is low.

What's Next?

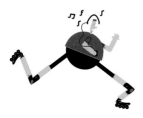

At this point, you've figured it out: you have seen the enemy, and that enemy is you. You know where your stress is coming from and how to pick it out of a lineup. So move on to Chapter 3, where we'll get down to business and learn how to manage the stress we've uncovered.

Attacking Stress in General

FAST FORWARD

Managing Stress in General ➤ *p. 33*
Constant change is a given. To handle it effectively, you must:
- Recognize what you can change.
- Become aware of your emotional reaction to stress.
- Reduce your emotional response to stress.
- Moderate your physical response to stress.
- Boost your physical reserves.
- Boost your emotional reserves.

How to Tell if You're Overdoing It ➤ *p. 35*
- You complain about how much you have to do and you feel that what you do is never enough.
- Life seems out of control.
- At the end of the day you feel out of control.

Dealing with Stress in General ➤ *p. 36*
There are a number of responses to help deal with stressful situations:
1. Keep yourself healthy.
2. Build a strong support system.
3. Don't forget to have fun.
4. Work on your self-esteem.
5. Learn how to communicate with others.
6. Learn coping skills.
7. Reframe.

Do Others Stress You Out? ➤ *p. 36*
To keep stressful relationships to a minimum:
- Be positive.
- Look your best.

- Be assertive.
- Give credit.

How's Your Primary Relationship? ➤ *p. 37*

Marriage is the perfect antidote to stress-related disease.

Your Kids and Stress ➤ *p. 37*

Children are a great joy and a great source of potential stress. Tips for keeping stress to a minimum:
- Accept your kids as *they* are.
- Allow them to learn from you and then go their own way.
- Understand that parenthood is not about control, it's about freedom.

It's Up to You ➤ *p. 38*

Stress won't disappear if you ignore it. To get a grip on life circumstances and avoid excess stress:
- Solve the problem.
- Adapt to the problem.
- Accept that it can't be changed.

Biofeedback ➤ *p. 38*

Biofeedback can be a useful tool in stress management. A biofeedback system allows you to monitor stress reactions in your body by watching the response from electronic sensors as you try to relax. Biofeedback allows you to monitor stress by measuring:
- Skin temperature changes
- Sweat on your skin
- Blood pressure changes

Know When to Get Help ➤ *p. 39*

Excess stress can affect your health, the way you think about your job, and even your personality. A mental health professional can help you deal with stress. Here are signs that your stress has reached crisis proportions and you may need professional help:

- You feel depressed most of the time (see Chapter 2).
- You are violent.
- You're getting too strict with your kids.
- You feel constantly let down by yourself or your family.
- You've been drinking more than usual.
- You get mean when you drink.
- You feel you can't cope.
- You're starting to lie to people about what you're doing.

A world without any stress at all would be a pretty boring place. Deadlines, confrontations, competition—all these challenges can add depth and color to our lives. The goal should not be to totally eliminate stress, but to learn how to manage it and use it effectively. In this chapter, you'll learn how to handle stress and change your reaction to it.

HABITS & STRATEGIES

Live in the here and now instead of in the past or future. Take note of what is happening now instead of being anxious about what might happen in the future. Focus on what is happening now instead of on the situation that occurred an hour ago.

Managing Stress in General

The key to managing stress depends a bit on how much of a magician you are—how much you can transform yourself and the life around you. If you tend to plod along with your eyes on the road and your hands in your pockets, you're going to have a harder time fending off life's slings and arrows. If you see that stress is taking a toll on your life, it's up to you to do something about it. You need to recognize, first of all, that the way you size up a situation is more important than the reality of the situation itself. Your *perception* of the situation fuels your response.

Constant change—and resultant stress—is pretty much a given these days. Anyone who has ever bought an expensive top-of-the-line computer only to see it become obsolete in a month is intimately acquainted with change. It is how you respond to that change that makes all the difference.

Recognize What You Can Change

- Can you avoid or eliminate the stressors?
- If not, can you lessen their intensity?
- Can you take a break or leave the event?

Become Aware of Your Emotional Reaction to Stress

- Notice your symptoms. Don't gloss over the tension.
- What events do you find stressful?
- How does your body respond to stress?

Change your perception and attitude toward time. Learn how to handle time and the stress it causes, and you can take the first steps toward reducing its impact on your health.

Reduce Your Emotional Response to Stress

- Do you think of your stressors in an overblown way?
- Are you trying to please everyone?
- Do you overreact?
- Try to see the stress as something you can cope with instead of something that overpowers you.
- Don't belabor the what-ifs—temper your emotions.

Moderate Your Physical Response to Stress

- Bring your heart rate and breathing to normal with slow, deep breaths.
- Reduce muscle tension with relaxation techniques.
- Biofeedback may help you gain voluntary control over your body.

Boost Your Physical Reserves

- Eat healthy.
- Exercise three times a week.
- Avoid nicotine, caffeine, and other stimulants.
- Take breaks; include leisure time in your day.
- Get enough rest.

More than 75 percent of the general population experiences at least some stress every two weeks. Half of those folks experience moderate or high levels of stress.

Boost Your Emotional Reserves

- Build a strong emotional support system.
- Expect some frustration and failure; that's why they call it "work."

- Pursue realistic goals that you want.
- Be a friend to yourself.

How to Tell if You're Overdoing It

We all occasionally feel stress, and there's nothing inherently wrong with that. How we handle that stress can make all the difference:

Tranquilizers, antidepressants, and antianxiety medications account for one-fourth of all prescriptions written in the United States each year.

- You complain about how much you have to do . . .

  Healthy response: You wouldn't want to completely give up one of your roles.

  Stressed out: You feel that what you do is never enough or is unfulfilling.

- Life seems . . .

  Healthy response: Challenging and full of potential.

  Stressed out: Out of control. When you look ahead, you believe nothing is going to change for the better.

- At the end of the day . . .

  Healthy response: "My to-do list is under control and I'm not ready to kill my boss."

  Stressed out: "I'm out of control and I can't take it any more!"

DEFINITION

80/20 principle: Only 20 percent of the tasks we do produce 80 percent of the results.

HABITS & STRATEGIES

Smile and acknowledge people. Notice everything that is around you instead of focusing on angry, negative thoughts. If you were to die in the next instant, would you want to be fuming over the idiot in the car ahead, or appreciating the beauty of the world?

Dealing with Stress in General

In general, you have a number of responses to help deal with stressful situations.

1. Keep yourself healthy so you can handle stress better.

2. Build a strong support system of friends and relatives.

3. Make sure you don't forget to have fun.

4. Work on your self-esteem. The more you think of yourself, the harder it will be to get beaten down by stress.

5. Learn how to communicate with others. The more you can touch other human beings, the less chance there will be for miscommunication and stress.

6. Learn coping skills: meditation, visualization, relaxation, biofeedback.

7. Reframe. Presidents aren't the only ones who can use spin doctors. Put problems in perspective and try to put a positive spin on the situation.

HABITS & STRATEGIES

While waiting in line, try to enjoy the process instead of getting frustrated and angry. Observe your posture; feel yourself connected to the earth. Do deep-breathing exercises.

Do Others Stress You Out?

Good relationships with others can be very satisfying, but nothing can drive you around the bend quicker than having unpleasant, stressful interactions with others. If you want to keep stressful relationships with others to a minimum:

- *Be positive.* People like to work with optimistic, happy people. If a problem presents itself, a positive approach can make the difference between success and failure.

- *Look your best.* Present a confident, open posture. Wear clean, good-quality clothes that project the image you want.

- *Be assertive.* You don't have to be a bully—just confidently project your right to have your views taken into account. If you hide in a corner you won't be noticed and your needs won't be met.
- *Give credit.* If someone else has done well, acknowledge that sincerely.

HABITS & STRATEGIES

Always leave people happy that they've spoken to you.

Only 14 percent of people during each decade of life up to age 70 will get heart disease from high blood pressure, high cholesterol, and smoking. One of the counterbalancing forces is marriage.

Walking in Their Topsiders

One of the best ways to avoid building up stressful relationships is to put yourself in other people's shoes—not only taking into account the present, but thinking about where they came from and what baggage they may be bringing forward from their childhoods.

If you have a friend who always calculates the tip to the third decimal point when you split the lunch bill, think about his or her childhood. Did he grow up poor in a family of 10? Did he have to work to put his three siblings through college? Did she have to support an alcoholic mother? Understanding a person's real motivations can go a long way toward making us more sympathetic.

How's Your Primary Relationship?

Would you like to slice your risk of all forms of illness, accident, and death in half? Here's one answer: get married. Of course, there's a downside to this. Just as being married is an antidote to stress-related disease, losing a spouse to death is a terrible blow and opens the door to illness. Researchers believe it's caused in large part by the stress of the grief response.

Your Kids and Stress

Having children is both a great joy and a great source of potential stress, all wrapped up in one. In order to keep your own stress muted to a dull roar, you need to:

- Accept your kids *as they are,* even if it means tolerating purple hair and a ring through the nose.
- Allow them to learn from you and then go their own way.
- Understand that parenthood is not about control, it's about freedom.

It's Up to You

In the next chapters, you'll learn specific strategies to conquer stress. In the end, stress is pretty much inevitable. You don't avoid getting sick by shouting "No!" each time a germ breaks through your defenses. Likewise, you won't outrun stress by shouting "No!" each time you meet a challenging circumstance. Instead, you have a choice:

- Solve the problem.
- Adapt to the problem.
- Accept that it can't be changed.

Biofeedback

In your search to manage your stress, biofeedback can be a useful tool, especially if you're intrigued by technical bells and whistles. You can participate in biofeedback training under the guidance of a hospital or university program, or you can try a version of it at home. (For example, you can purchase devices to measure your own blood pressure.)

A biofeedback system uses electronic sensors to measure stress in your body and send the results to you. The system may use a pen on a graph, a pitch of sound, a light, and so on. This lets you experiment with stress management techniques and actually see them take effect.

Biofeedback can be especially effective for people who may be uncomfortable with the hard-to-quantify relaxation methods of imagery, visualization, and meditation. The system converts vague feelings into hard, observable information that can help you fine-tune your stress management technique. It's especially helpful if you have a stress-related condition, including high blood pressure, anxiety, or migraine headaches.

The Technical Stuff . . .

Basically, biofeedback works like this:

- You get hooked up to a machine that measures an unconscious activity (blood pressure, pulse, body temperature, muscle tension, sweat, brain waves, or stomach acidity).
- As you practice some version of relaxation, you get feedback (that's where the name comes from) about your body from the machine via a light, a moving needle, or something similar.
- After some practice, you can learn to associate how you feel with your internal body process. For example, you get to know how it feels when your blood pressure rises.
- After even more practice (this method is useful only to very dedicated people!), you can learn to lower your blood pressure yourself using a variety of techniques.

Stress contributes to the development of alcoholism, obesity, suicide, drug addiction, cigarette addiction, and other harmful behaviors.

CAUTION

Know When to Get Help

When stress builds up, it can affect your health, the way you think about your job, and even your personality.

A mental health professional can help you handle your stress and fears, as well as plan for the future. If you can't afford mental health care, your minister, priest, or rabbi may provide counseling at no cost to you. The following are signs that your stress has reached crisis proportions and you need professional help:

- *You feel depressed most of the time (see Chapter 2).*
- *You are violent toward your family.*
- *You become too strict with your kids.*
- *You feel constantly let down by yourself or your family.*
- *You've been drinking more than usual.*
- *You get mean when you drink.*
- *You feel you can't cope.*
- *You're starting to lie to people about what you're doing.*

How Biofeedback Works

- *Skin temperature measures:* When you're stressed, adrenaline diverts blood from your body surface to the interior of your body in preparation for flight or fight. As less warm blood is available at the surface, skin temperature drops.
- *Skin electrical activity:* When you're stressed, you sweat more (as anyone knows who has ever had to ask somebody out on a date). Skin that is damp conducts electricity more effectively than dry skin. This type of biofeedback measures the amount of electricity conducted between two electrodes.
- *Blood pressure:* When you're under stress, blood pressure rises. Because some people have extremely high blood pressure without appearing to be stressed, biofeedback using this measure is good for those trying to lower high blood pressure.

DEFINITION

biofeedback: A technique in which a person uses information about a normally unconscious body function (such as blood pressure) to gain conscious control over that function.

CAUTION

Don't keep anger, anxiety and stress bottled up. Share your tension with your partner or a close friend.

What's Next?

Next stop: attacking those stressful thoughts, behaviors, and attitudes.

Attacking Stressful Thoughts and Behavior

FAST FORWARD

Personality and Stress ➤ *p. 45*

Your personality can influence your stress level. In addition to type
As, the following personality types can cause stress:

- The perfectionist
- The martyr

Beliefs and Expectations ➤ *p. 47*

The unconscious beliefs we have about the world and about
ourselves can be potent causes of stress. We can learn to tell the
difference between innate truth and opinion. Expectations we
have about ourselves and others also may be untrue. Allow
yourself to make mistakes. Try as hard as you can, and don't be
too negative.

Taking Control ➤ *p. 49*

People who are stressed aren't usually in control of their lives.
Being in control is largely a matter of attitude. You can decide to
take control of your life by anticipating problems before they occur.
At the same time, you can work on personal and self-improvement
goals to alleviate even more stress.

Reframing ➤ *p. 50*

There are always many ways to look at any given situation.
Choose to reframe the situation in a positive light and you can
ease much of the stress that's associated with it. Use reframing to
handle not just work/home situations, but difficult people
problems as well.

Keeping Things in Perspective ➤ *p. 51*

You need to keep things in perspective if you want to get a handle on stress. Ask yourself:

- Is this really a problem?
- Has anyone else ever had this problem?
- Can I split the problem in smaller parts?
- What are my priorities?
- What's the worst that could happen?

Negative Thinking ➤ *p. 52*

Negative thinking can be a big stress builder, turning every opportunity into a chance for failure. Negative thinking comes in a variety of packages.

- *All or nothing thinking:* If you make one mistake, you're a failure.
- *Overgeneralizing:* If you lost out on a promotion, you'll never get another one.
- *Personalizing:* You must be the cause of everyone else's bad moods or problems.

Thought Awareness ➤ *p. 54*

One way to get a handle on negative thoughts is to simply become aware of them. Write them down and decide rationally whether they really have a basis in reality. If simply noticing them isn't enough, work on replacing negative thoughts with positive ones. Give yourself positive affirmations to change negative thoughts into positive ones.

- I can achieve my goals.
- I can do this.
- I am completely self-confident in every social situation.

Anticipating Stress ➤ p. 56

You can surmount stress by figuring out where it's coming from and then preparing an action plan to survive it.

- Analyze the likely source of your stress.
- Rehearse your response.
- If you can't beat it, try to avoid it.

Handling Depression ➤ p. 57

High levels of stress can lead to clinical depression. Serious depression requires medical treatment. You may be depressed if one or more of the following are true:

- You feel terribly sad or cry a lot.
- You gain or lose weight, binge, or overeat.
- You sleep too little or not enough and feel tired all the time.
- You lose interest in sex or activities you once enjoyed.
- You feel guilty, unattractive, unworthy.
- You have trouble concentrating.
- You brood and have phobias, delusions, or fears.
- You have thoughts about suicide.

Most people think of stress as something that happens *to* them. But how you approach life—your beliefs, your thoughts, and your attitude—can have a major impact on long-term stress management. If you always look at your glass as half empty, you're already halfway down the road to Stressville—you've set yourself up for stress by expecting it. When your attitude is negative or hostile, you won't see the opportunities, because you are automatically making problems out of every situation. Your attitude can cause more stress by alienating and irritating others. In this chapter, you'll learn all the ways your mental outlook contributes to stress—and how to improve that outlook.

Personality

It shouldn't come as a surprise to you that your personality can influence your level of stress. We've all known the typical type A personality, who thrives on stress, and the type B, who has a more mellow approach to life. You may not be aware that other personality traits can also cause stress:

- *The perfectionist:* This is someone whose impossibly high standards are so excessive no one could ever meet them. Constantly striving for perfection—and constantly failing—is a leading cause of stress.

- *The martyr:* Moms have gotten a bad rap for this one, but anyone can be so self-effacing that he is always looking to the needs of others—and then is unhappy when no one looks after his needs.

Stress-Building Personality Test

Are You a Perfectionist?

- Do you feel constant pressure to achieve?
- Do you feel you haven't done enough, no matter what you do?
- Are you hard on yourself when you find out you're not perfect?
- Do you drive yourself to be the best in what you do, giving up everything in the pursuit of perfection?

Are You a Control Freak?

- Do you feel the need to be in control of everything and everyone?
- Do you think lack of control is a sign of weakness?
- Do you run your life by lists?
- Are you reluctant to delegate to others?

Are You a People Pleaser?

- Do you need to have everyone like you?
- Do you feel upset if someone doesn't like you?
- Do you care more for others than you do for yourself?
- Do you hide your negative feelings so as not to displease others?

Do You Feel Incompetent?

- Do you feel that you have poor judgment?
- Do you feel you lack common sense?
- Do you feel like an imposter?
- Do you feel that you don't do as good a job as others?

If you answer yes to any of these questions, you could have a potential problem there. More than two yeses in any one area indicates a real roadblock.

Beliefs

You may not realize it, but you're a walking compendium of beliefs—and many of them are real stress builders. Lots of these beliefs have an implied "shall" that may or may not be true but that carry along a lot of baggage. These beliefs might include the following:

- You can't fight city hall.
- Children should be seen and not heard.
- Men never cry.
- Women can't [fill in the blank].

We also have beliefs about ourselves—an unconscious list of traits and faults that we drag along from childhood. "I just don't like social situations." "I can't remember details." "I'm just not neat." Most of our beliefs are unconscious, and this gives them tremendous power. They shape our lives and mold our destiny, and we may never know their names.

Your beliefs cause stress because they drive your behavior. The person who believes that "something worth doing is worth doing well" may drive herself relentlessly to fulfill this creed. Someone who says "If you want something done right, you have to do it yourself" is most likely not a good delegator.

But are they truths, or are they just opinions?

Beliefs and Other People

Beliefs also cause stress when they make us collide head-on into other people. You may have a big fight with your husband because he didn't change the sheets every week: "Everyone changes the sheets every week," you tell him. Where does this idea come form? "Everybody knows it. My mother taught me."

In fact, it is not an immutable law that you must change the sheets every week. In some cultures, sheets are changed only once a month. Believing there is an immutable law that "everyone" knows can cause stress until you acknowledge that it's really just your preference.

1. Articulate your beliefs.

2. Label them as beliefs and not as truths.

3. Admit these opinions can be changed.

4. Admit beliefs held by someone else may be just as valid.

Unrealistic Expectations and Stress

The person who holds unrealistic desires is the person who is going to be drowning in stress. You may become upset at something not because it's inherently stressful, but because it doesn't coincide with your expectations. You may be able to handle regular rush-hour traffic, for example, but when you're in a hurry to get to your son's picnic and you get stuck in an unexpected Sunday traffic jam, it causes stress.

Many people have held at least one of the following unrealistic expectations at one time or another:

1. "I always want to have the love and admiration of everybody who is important to me." *Remember,* it's completely unrealistic to expect everyone to love you, because you have no control over what other people think or feel.

2. "I want to be completely competent at all times." *Remember,* the only way you're going to get good at things you can't do now is to make mistakes. Everybody does.

3. "Factors outside myself cause all stress and problems." *Remember,* negative situations are often caused by your own negative attitudes. The Eastern religious leaders teach that *thoughts are things.* Your own negative attitudes can make you see neutral events in a negative light, and the more negatively you think about things, the more negative they become.

4. "I want events always to turn out the way I want them to, and I want people always to do what I want." *Remember,* other people have their own ideas and their own agendas. You can't control that.

5. "Past bad experience will always control what will happen in the future." *Remember,* most of the time you can change or improve things if you try hard enough or look at a problem differently. The only sure thing is that if you do nothing, nothing will change.

Taking Control

The difference between being in control and being out of control is just a little bit of advance planning.

Unrealistic expectations cause stress because they make life feel unpredictable and out of control. If you know you have to work late, you can plan for it; if your boss just drops in at the last minute and orders you to stay, it's going to cause stress.

People who feel monumentally stressed are usually not in control of their lives—or at least they are not in control of that particular situation. In fact, the feeling of being out of control is stressful all by itself, notwithstanding all the other stresses there are.

You'll be happy to know that being in control is largely a matter of attitude.

If you decide to take control of your life, you can anticipate the problems that lead to stress. When you spend your time rushing around stamping out brush fires and worrying about the next conflagration that's going to come roaring over the hill, how can you have time to relax and enjoy life?

Here's a typical stressful morning:

- The dress you planned to wear to the meeting today is at the cleaners. You have nothing else to wear.
- There's no bread to make your daughter's sandwich for school.
- The cat is out of cat food and screaming for breakfast.
- You're out of gas and you're late for work.

Each one of these scenarios adds more stress—and the day has hardly begun. A bit of advance panning could avert every single one of those problems.

1. Once a week, sit down (Friday night is good) and go over your schedule for the following week. (This gives you time to purchase supplies if you're low.)

2. Take clothes to the dry cleaner and make sure laundry is done by Monday for that week. You'll never be short of clothes.

3. Add all needed grocery items (including bread and cat food) to the list so you have enough for the week.

4. Make it a policy to fill up your car with gas *every* Sunday, whether or not the gas gauge is on "E."

Some people like to spend January 1 working on long-term goals for the upcoming year. This is a good time for reflection and optimistic goal setting.

Taking the time to go over the week's events—plan a bit in advance—needn't take more than 10 minutes. But you'll be surprised how much more streamlined your days will be.

Self-Improvement Goals

You might also take the time to add some goal-setting and self-improvement objectives while you're compiling your weekly list. Sometimes needless stress is caused by our unique personality traits. If you tend to be pessimistic and focused on faults, pick one problem to work on during the coming week.

Once a month (perhaps the first of the month or the first Friday of the month) you can work on longer-term goals. What would you like to accomplish by next month, next year, within five years? If you never spend time thinking about these long-term goals, the months and years will slip by so fast you'll never have a chance to plan for the future that so quickly becomes the present.

Reframing

When you're embroiled in stressful situations you lose the ability to see what you're doing that can make things worse. Reframing is a technique to change the way you look at things so you'll feel better about them.

The key to becoming a successful reframer is to understand that there are *always* many different ways to look at any situation. Reality may be unchanging, but there are different ways to perceive that reality. You might as well pick the one that's going to cause you the least stress.

You can do this by seeing the positives in every negative situation, or at least by entertaining thoughts about how something might be perceived differently.

Let's say you just lost your job. Can you find the upside to this?

- Maybe you really hated the job anyway, but never had the courage to leave. Now you'll have a chance to explore something you might like better.
- The experience of finding a new job is scary, but we never grow when we're not challenged. This could make you a stronger person.
- You'll have to watch your spending more carefully—something that you've never done before. There is a real chance for discipline and growth here.

You can use reframing not just to ease the stress of a situation at home or work, but to handle people as well. Suppose your coworker drives you crazy because she is always trying to be superior. How could you reframe that behavior?

- She is probably insecure.
- She may be worried that you will eclipse her. By trying to put you down, she is hoping to rise above you.
- She may be having personal problems.
- She may resent you for reasons that have nothing to do with you at all.

Keeping Things in Perspective

When the widgets are flying down that conveyor belt or your in-basket is threatening to take over your desk, it's pretty easy to lose perspective. Before you know it, you've entered the stress zone where every problem puts on more pressure, which makes you more stressed, which magnifies every problem, which makes you more stressed . . .

Even hamsters get off that treadmill once in a while, and you should, too. Fortunately, there are ways to slam on the brakes when you find yourself in this downward spiral. . . . Ask yourself the following questions:

1. *Is this really a problem?*
   - Sometimes a problem is just an opportunity for you to do something well.
   - If it really is a problem, most other people wouldn't do any better than you're doing.
   - If you manage to deal with it, what a triumph for you!
   - If you face this problem, what will you learn from it no matter what happens?

2. *Has anybody else ever had this problem?*
   - Talk to your mentors at work, people more experienced than you. How have they handled such a problem?
   - If others have experienced the problem, discuss it and see if you can brainstorm some solutions.

*If you've done your best
and you've learned from the
mistake, you can't do any
better than that.*

3. *Can I divide this problem into workable pieces?*
   - Even the biggest, most horrible task can be divided into smaller, more manageable portions. Imagine how the Egyptians felt when they were planning the pyramids! If they could do it, you can, too.

4. *What are my priorities?*
   - You've got 23 tasks to do before noon tomorrow. When you get over the initial horror, calm down and look at them rationally. Some of them are very important, and some can be put off.
   - List the jobs in descending order of importance. For those jobs that seem fairly unimportant, take a page from Scarlett O'Hara's notebook and "think about them tomorrow."

5. *What's the worst that could happen?*
   - In 10 years, will the fact that you were two days late with the Walters' report really matter? Will it matter in 20 years? In a lifetime?
   - Even if it *did* matter, most likely you'll have other opportunities to correct the mistake or blossom in other ways.

Distorted, Negative Thinking

Ever been in a room with a negative thinker? This is a person who constantly puts himself down, criticizes herself for errors, doubts his abilities, expects failure. The little black cloud hanging over the negative thinker's head virtually guarantees a lifetime of stress.

Negative thinking is the flip side of optimism—it destroys confidence, interferes with your performance, and slows down your mental skills. It's a stress generator. Negative thinking comes in a variety of packages, and all of them are pretty destructive.

Examples of Negative Thoughts

- "I should have put on lipstick. I always look so badly groomed . . ."
- "I'm terrible at public speaking. If I don't do well I'll never get that promotion."
- "I'm so bad at meeting new people."

- "All these guys are so successful. What am I doing here?"
- "I don't deserve this job. I wonder how soon they're going to find out that I'm a fake and that I got this job on a fluke?"

Are You an All-or-Nothing Thinker?

Either you're the best commodity options dealer in the world, or you're a poor misguided chump who couldn't sell a Beanie Baby to a second grader. You snapped at your son, so you've got to be the worst parent in the world. It's all or nothing. It's not really so.

Instead, realize that the truth is, even Bill Gates crashes his computer sometimes, and even Mary Lou Retton had days when she fell off the pommel horse. You can't be defined by any single act, and one mistake doesn't usually destroy an entire project.

Overgeneralizing

A second cousin to the all-or-nothing thinker is the person who overgeneralizes, who sees every mistake as part of a dark and twisted pattern of inevitable failure. If you think this way, then when you fail to land that job you'll see this as just one more piece of evidence that you'll never get a job.

Instead, evaluate each incident on its own merits. If you've missed out on the last four jobs you've interviewed for, find out what you might be doing wrong instead of giving up in despair.

Personalizing

This is the favorite ploy of people who walk around attracting guilt like a magnet. Have you ever walked in the door, been greeted curtly by the boss, and then spent the next three hours obsessing in your office about what you did wrong—only to find out that the boss had a fight with his wife that morning and was just out of sorts?

If you do, you're not alone. Many, many people tend to read all sorts of slights in a very personal manner, and the more sensitive you are, the more likely you are to personalize.

Instead, the right response is to say nothing. If you really *did* anger your boss, most likely he or she will let you know.

Thought Awareness

All the negative thought distortions we discussed are just that—distortions. They're evidence of a mind gone out of control, running free down that road to negative self-destruction.

You'd be surprised how often people have no idea what's running through their heads. It's sort of like being on autopilot; once you stop and pay attention to what thoughts are streaming through your mind, it's an eye-opening experience.

Those moments when you're under stress are a good time to practice thought awareness, because this is when you're most likely to have spontaneous negative thoughts running rampant. Normally, these negative clinkers appear and disappear without being noticed. Here's what you should do:

1. Observe your thoughts.
2. Don't suppress them—just observe them as they run their course.
3. Be on the lookout for negative thoughts while you're observing this stream of consciousness.

Rational Thinking

Once you're aware of your negative thoughts, write them down. Look them over and ask yourself honestly whether they have any basis in truth. Odds are, they don't, because negative self-talk doesn't spring from our rational minds—it comes from those dark and creepy corners of our psyche where all our deepest fears are hiding.

Once you've examined these negative thoughts, you're in a position to attack them logically. Once you do this, you may find that they lose their power and eventually disappear. Often, negative thoughts persist only because they aren't routinely noticed.

Positive Thinking

If simply noticing or acknowledging them doesn't do the trick, you may have to take some stronger action. First, you need to replace negative thoughts with positive ones.

Negative thought:	"I'll never get this project done on time."
Positive spin:	"I'll concentrate on one thing at a time. I'll make steady progress."
Negative thought:	"I can't believe I made that accounting mistake on page 10. I've disappointed everyone."
Positive thought:	"No one is perfect. I did my best. The overall report is fine."

Replacing negative thoughts with positive ones takes practice. When you catch yourself with a negative thought, review the evidence. Is there another way to look at the situation?

Positive Affirmations

You can always counter your negative thoughts with positive affirmations. These positive affirmations can build confidence and change negative behavior patterns into positive ones.

The key is to base your affirmations on a rational assessment of fact and use them to fight against the negative thinking that might have undermined your self-confidence. Here are some handy positive affirmations you might consider using:

- I can achieve my goals.
- I can do this.
- I am completely self-confident in every social situation.
- I am completely myself, and people will like me.
- I am in control of my life.
- I am a valued person.

Using positive affirmations can give you surprising strength, but it isn't a panacea. It's not likely that simply telling yourself you're an Olympic diver of supreme ability will turn you into a Greg Louganis. (But odds are good that Greg Louganis thinks fairly positive thoughts.) You need to have a balanced outlook here. Decide rationally what goals you can realistically reach with hard work. Use positive thinking to reinforce those goals.

For more information on positive affirmations, see Chapter 7.

Anticipating Stress

The best way to head off stress is to figure out where it's going to be coming from before it happens. This kind of preemptive strike gives you power and a feeling of self-control. If you know what's going to be coming, you can plan ahead to at least reduce stress from an ambush. You can prepare for stress in a number of ways:

- Rehearse. If you've got your flipcharts and your laser pointer but you're still nervous about a presentation, run through the event in your mind until you feel your performance is polished. You'll still feel stress, but at least you'll be confident.
- Worrying never got anybody out of a hole. Analyzing the likely cause of stress and then planning your response can either alleviate the situation or help you cope with it when it comes.
- Avoid it. It's not necessarily the coward's way out. Sometimes, the only way to beat a stressful, unpleasant situation is simply to step aside and refuse to confront it. Only you can decide if you can get away with it.

Don't Rely Too Much on Expectations of Others

In a perfect world, we'd all obey the speed limit, never lie about our weight on our driver's license, and never cheat at Monopoly. But people don't always behave the way you expect them to. Your son gets his nose pierced. Life-long Republicans vote for Clinton. That cretin in accounting took credit for your idea.

Getting wound up because someone else hasn't met your expectations won't make the stress any easier to take. If you accept that sometimes your expectations won't be met, you can move through the stress and find a solution to the problem.

Expect less from people who are likely to disappoint you. It makes coping easier and less upsetting that way.

Controlling Uncertainty

There's nothing worse than sitting at your desk in a new job and not having a clue about what to do next. Struggling with uncertainty can cause high levels of stress. You don't know what to do, but surely if you ask you'll look incompetent.

The first step is to analyze where your uncertainty comes from:

- Do you wonder what your boss thinks of your abilities?
- Do you believe you've received vague, inconsistent instructions?
- Are you unsure where your organization is going?
- Do you worry about what will be expected from you in the future?

If you analyze these questions, you'll see that in each case your inability to perform is caused by either a lack of information or the actions of other people. It doesn't take a rocket scientist to see the solution to this one: ask for the information you need.

- If you don't know how you're measuring up, sit down with your boss and ask for a performance review. Your boss will be pleased to see you care.
- It's much better to ask for clarification than to keep silent and make mistakes. Keep asking for clarification until you know exactly what you're doing.
- If you're unclear about your organization's future, sit down with your boss—or your boss's boss. You're a part of the organization, so you have a right to know.
- You need to know what your boss expects from you in the future so you can make appropriate career decisions. You can ask this question when you have a performance review.

Handling Depression

Depression is a common result of having to cope with high levels of stress for a long time or during life crises.

CAUTION

Severe depression is a clinical illness that should be treated medically. It's nothing to be ashamed of, but it must be taken seriously. Odds are, you won't just snap out of it. Severe depression can be treated quite successfully with a combination of medication and counseling.

While depression is a medical illness and may be in part genetic, there are often triggers in vulnerable people. You may begin to experience severe depression in these situations:

- You are passed over for promotion.
- You miss important deadlines.
- You lose an important business deal.
- You feel inadequate to handle a new difficult job.
- You are bored for a long time.

Sometimes people who are depressed don't like to admit they have a problem. If you answer yes to more than one or two of the following questions, you could have a problem with depression:

- Do you feel terribly sad or cry a lot?
- Have you gained or lost weight? Do you binge or overeat?
- Do you have chronic insomnia or excessive sleepiness? Are you tired all the time?
- Do you have outbursts of complaints or shouting? Do you feel resentful or angry most of the time?
- Have you lost interest in activities you once enjoyed?
- Have you lost interest in sex?
- Do you feel guilty, unworthy, unattractive?
- Do you have trouble concentrating? Are your thoughts muddy?
- Do you brood and have phobias, delusions, or great fears?
- Have you thought you'd be better off dead?

Support Systems

A problem shared is a problem halved.

When the stress builds up, having someone to turn to can have profound effects on your health. If you have a live-in partner, great. Friends and family also count, as long as the relationship is fairly positive. Pets are good, and so are religious organizations and other groups. If you don't have a solid support system, you should buy one—some type of mental health counselor.

In fact, the value of social support is so strong, studies have found that counseling alone—without modifying diet or exercise at all—can reduce the risk of heart attacks.

What's Next?

Now we're off to everyone's favorite topic: stress on the job and how to deal with it.

CHAPTER

5

Stress on the Job

INCLUDES

- Are you stressed?
- Audit your stress
- Make an action plan to conquer stress
- Balance work and leisure
- Eliminate environmental stress
- Commuting stress
- Business travel stress

FAST FORWARD

Is Your Job Stress Killing You? ➤ p. 66

Here's how to tell if your job stress is taking its toll:

- Is it hard to get up in the morning?
- Are you always tired?
- Do you forget things?
- Do you have aches and pains?
- Are you less interested in hobbies?
- Do you often feel angry?

Do a Stress Audit ➤ p. 66

Make a list of everything that bothers you about your job. Focus on the problems you can fix, and live with or avoid the rest.

Make an Action Plan to Conquer Stress ➤ p. 66

Work out a detailed plan to manage your stress.

- Manage your time.
- Make to-do lists.
- Avoid time wasters.
- Take a time-out.
- Pace yourself.
- Schedule breaks.
- Delegate.

Sense of Control Is Vital ➤ p. 70

People who don't have much sense of control over their jobs, no matter how much responsibility they have, are apt to be the most stressed. This section includes a list of the top 10 most and least stressful jobs.

Balance Work and Leisure ➤ *p. 72*

Do you spend too much time at work and not enough at home? Chart the balance between your work and leisure, and see if you're spending too much time in any one area:

- Work
- Family
- Community
- Self

Environmental Stress on the Job ➤ *p. 72*

The physical surroundings of your job can contribute greatly to your stress:

- Make sure your office air is healthy.
- Keep the noise level under control.
- Confirm that your desk and chair are comfortable and correct for the job.
- Make certain your computer monitor is located in the proper place.
- See that you have adequate and correct lighting.
- Type and sit in the correct posture.

Don't Let Stress Affect Your Sleep ➤ *p. 78*

If your job is giving you insomnia:

- Don't use sleeping pills.
- Exercise a few hours before bedtime.
- Eat lightly; avoid caffeine.
- Take a warm bath right before bedtime.
- Listen to soothing music in bed.
- Don't sleep late on weekends.

Commuting Stress ➤ *p. 80*

A long commute can be a real stress inducer. Try to avoid peak travel times, join a carpool if possible, play tapes to distract yourself, use public transportation if possible.

Business Travel Stress ➤ *p. 81*

If you have to travel a lot for business:

- Keep a to-do list and finish everything three days before you leave.
- Keep a bag always packed and ready to go.
- Minimize time-zone jet lag.

You don't have to be an air traffic controller to have lots of stress on the job. Despite modern technology with all its labor-saving devices, it's not getting any better: the workplace is the leading source of stress for most adults. Whether you're staffing a medical lab, typing up reports, or waiting on tables, the world of work is a world of stress. In fact, being satisfied with your job is the number one predictor for long life—more important than how healthy you are, whether you smoke, or what genes you've inherited.

You'd think that with modern technology all our jobs would be much easier to take, but it's just not so. For example, the advent of the computer didn't make a secretary's job any easier. Now the ease of editing means that your boss won't think twice about having you rewrite letters 10 times or more. They can be filed away and just rewritten, over and over again.

In this chapter, we'll be looking at job stress in all its permutations and discussing what can be done about easing some of the headaches. Many of us are plunged into stress long before we ever even *get* to the office by virtue of a long commute.

CAUTION

Job stress can be unhealthy for pregnant women. In one study of 600 women lawyers, those who worked more than 45 hours a week were more than three times as likely to experience miscarriages as those who worked less than 35 hours a week.

The average executives sit at their desks for one-third of their lives. Shouldn't you make it a point to spend that time in a pleasurable way?

Are You Stressed?

Not everyone believes that they are stressed on the job, even in the presence of significant symptoms. How many of these situations do you have on your job?

- *Too much or too little work*
- *Having to surmount unnecessary obstacles*
- *Time pressures/deadlines*
- *Having to perform beyond your ability*
- *Keeping up with new technology*
- *Constantly changing procedures or policies*
- *Lack of clear job objectives*
- *No support or career advice*
- *Responsibility for personnel, budgets, or equipment but no control*

Career Development Stress

On your job, do you experience any of the following?

- *Boredom with your current job*
- *Lack of opportunity for advancement*
- *Lack of job security*
- *Glass ceiling*
- *Promotion beyond your ability*
- *Lack of promotion and boredom*
- *Frustration with your role*

Customer or Organization Stress

Do you think your stress could be coming from any of the following?

- *Meddling in your work*
- *Pressure from your boss*
- *Customer demands*
- *Telephone interruptions*

Is Your Job Stress Killing You?

Remember that you own your time. You may need to make concessions at work, but ultimately how you choose to spend your time is your decision.

Longer hours and more work spread among fewer workers because of corporate downsizing is bound to take its toll in stress-induced health problems. Here's how to tell if work stress may be harming your health:

- Do you have a hard time getting up?
- Are you always tired?
- Are you forgetting things?
- Do you have mysterious aches and pains?
- Have you lost your appetite?
- Are you less interested in your activities?
- Do you feel really irritable or angry?

We all have that occasional monster day, but if you logged more than three yeses to this quiz, you really need to do something about your work stress.

Do a Stress Audit

When work gets you down, get out a sheet of paper and write down everything that bothers you about your job. Do you hate the way you have to write down every paper clip you use? Does it drive you nuts when you have to sign out whenever you leave the building? Maybe your boss just doesn't know how to boss.

Now look over your list. Odds are, some problems you could fix and others would take an act of Congress to sort out. Focus on the ones you can rectify and avoid the others whenever possible.

Make an Action Plan to Conquer Stress

When you understand how much stress you can tolerate and where your job stress is coming from, then you can work out a plan to manage the stress. It should be detailed and contain ways to control or eliminate the stress you feel. Here's an example of an action plan:

1. Train Jane Smith to take over the Harris account.

2. Set work goals for what I want to accomplish this year.

3. Improve coordination with Suzy Brown.

4. Clean up my file area so I can find things more easily.

5. Buy an air filter for the office so the cigar smoke doesn't bother me.

6. Drink no more than two cups of coffee.

7. Take breaks every two hours.

8. Go to sleep by 10 P.M. every night.

As stress on the job builds up and the work reaches epic proportions, you may have to hurry up and finish your work in a slapdash fashion. It may escape the boss's notice, but *you* know you did the work poorly. This leads to frustration and a feeling of failure, which leads to more stress—and the whole unpleasant mess starts all over again.

The key to getting around this dead-end trap is to use good time management skills.

Manage Your Time Before It Manages You

If you're more in control of your time, you'll be more productive and you'll experience less stress on the job. The key to effective time management is to concentrate on *results,* not on activity.

Daily To-Do List

Make a daily to-do list and separate those things you *must* do, the things you *should* do, and the things you *want* to do.

1. Look over the "must" and the "should" list to determine whether you really need to do these things. Perhaps you could delegate them to someone else.

2. Once you've pared down the list, prioritize.

3. Don't try to complete everything at once.

4. Assign a date or time to accomplish each of the tasks. Don't be unrealistic; give yourself enough time.

Take Control of Time Wasters

There are a variety of other things you can do to take back control of your time:

- When you're struggling to get some work done, a ringing telephone can be the biggest time waster. If you don't have a secretary to screen your calls, rely on an answering machine to screen your calls. You're not obligated to answer the phone each time it rings.
- Establish a rule that when your door is closed, you're not to be disturbed, but when the door is open you're willing to stop what you're doing and brainstorm.
- Remember, you're not the only employee. Other people like to contribute; you don't need to be the only player.
- Recognize that there is a difference between being interested in quality work and being a perfectionist. Striving for perfection can waste time and create needless stress.
- Assess how you use your time. Keep a log for one day, recording how you spend each minute on the job. You'll soon see where you're wasting time and spinning your wheels.
- Create more time. If you have more jobs than time, try to come in 30 minutes early or leave 30 minutes later. Try carving 15 minutes off your lunch hour.

Pace Yourself

Even Michael Jordan wouldn't expect to race up and down the court for an entire game without a break. So why should you think it's perfectly reasonable to work from sunup to sundown without stopping for an intermission? Initially, stress may indeed boost your on-the-job performance. But once you pass a certain point, additional stress begins to hamper your ability to do a good job.

You cycle in and out of deep sleep every night. In the same way, you cycle in and out of productive periods during the day. Perhaps you've noticed that you tend to be a morning person with a midafternoon slump, or a slow starter who doesn't really get going until about 11 A.M. These cycles, called *ultradian rhythms,* happen all day long.

More than 51 percent of everyone between the ages of 35 and 54 report having a stressful job or feeling a great deal of stress.

To operate at peak efficiency, be on the lookout for those slothful troughs, and take a minibreak instead of plowing through them and building up stress.

Schedule Your Breaks

It may not be convenient to rush out of your job for an ultradian break. But most of us can divide the day into two-hour segments in this way:

- Midmorning break
- Lunch
- Midafternoon break
- Supper

On these breaks, don't just wolf down a bagel and cream cheese. Sit back and daydream. Go for a walk. Listen to music with your headphones. Meditate.

Delegate

If you have the luxury of an assistant, give her more work to do. Delegate—it will free you up to do what *you* do best.

If you don't have an assistant, see if you can turn to a coworker for help and then return the favor when she's two weeks behind on the profit and loss statement.

If you work for yourself, consider hiring a part-time assistant to come in and do the routine work so you can accomplish your overall business goals.

Sense of Control

Recent studies have shown that it's an employee's lack of control over the workplace, *not* whether there are three kinds of Snapple in the break room, that really causes job stress. Just how stressful can be shocking.

In fact, it's the Dilberts of the world who have the highest risk of heart disease in the workplace—a shocking 50 percent higher than the Mr. Bumsteads sitting in the executive suite. People in low-status jobs have worse health and die sooner, are more likely to smoke, and are less likely to exercise.

Too many times, employees have plenty of responsibility but little control over that responsibility. You may have to make sure that your department doesn't go over budget, but when it comes to actually deciding what those budget line items will be, your hands are tied.

Workers' compensation claims for "mental stress" in California rose between 200 and 700 percent in the 1980s. All other causes remained stable or declined.

Most Stressful Occupations

The National Institute of Occupational Safety and Health has put together a list of the most and least stressful occupations based on the incidence of stress-related problems such as heart and artery disease, high blood pressure, and nervous disorders.

Laborer
Secretary
Inspector
Clinical lab technician
Office manager
Foreman
Manager or administrator
Waitress or waiter
Machine operator
Farm owner
Miner or machine operator
Painter (not an artist)

Least Stressful Occupations

Seamstress (handstitcher)
Checker
Stock handler
Craftsman
Maid
Farm worker
Heavy-equipment operator
Freight handler
Child-care worker
Packer, wrapper
College professor
Personnel or labor relations worker

Balance Work and Leisure

Flextime notwithstanding, today's worker is slaving away for three more hours than we did 20 years ago—that adds up to one full extra month of work each year. And in far greater numbers than 20 years ago, both husband and wife are working outside the home, leaving little leisure time for relaxing family pursuits.

How is the balance at your house? Take a sheet of paper and divide it up as follows:

The main reason people don't have enough leisure time is that they can't bear to give themselves permission to do so.

- Work
- Family
- Community
- Self

How much time do you spend on each? If you're working more than 60 percent of the time or spending less than 10 percent on yourself, you could be heading for a stress breakdown.

Eliminate Environmental Stress on the Job

Would you rather sit down to work in a clean, neat office with everything in its place, or a crowded mess that looks more like a jumble sale at Lord & Taylor than a well-run office?

A well-organized, pleasant working environment can significantly reduce stress and boost productivity. If you have to spend 10 minutes searching through piles every time you need a new report, a box of pencils, or an important file, it's not surprising that you'll end up stressed out and lagging behind your deadlines.

Air Quality

Sick building syndrome is a condition in which an office building puts polluted air into the workers' environment. This can be caused by solvents in the carpets and furniture, asbestos fibers, air-conditioning molds and fungi, and so on. If the pollution is bad enough, it can make workers sick and boost stress.

You can do a number of things to improve the air quality of the place where you must spend eight hours every day:

- Open windows (if they will open).
- Ban smoking—at least in your own office if it's not possible elsewhere.
- Use a HEPA filter air purifier to remove 99 percent of pollutants.
- If humidity is a problem, bring in a portable dehumidifier (change and clean it often, or you'll have an additional source of pollutants).
- Fill your office with plants. They'll raise the level of oxygen, reduce stuffiness, and help raise humidity.

Excess Noise

Noise pollution can lead to significant work stress and, if it's loud enough, can damage your hearing over the long term. Even if you work in a business office, excess noise can be a problem—especially in an open-space office where everyone works in one room divided into cubicles. It's probably not loud enough to damage your hearing, but it is certainly loud enough to interfere with your concentration and raise your stress level.

The sound of people talking and laughing, office printers and computers, ringing phones, faxes, and copy machines, or of meetings going on all combine to raise the stress level. By the end of the day, you are probably going home tired, irritable, and tense.

If noise is a problem where you work, try these solutions:

- Install temporary partitions to divide the open space into cubicles.
- Use a separate conference room when you need to concentrate.
- Get everyone to use a separate meeting room away from the main office area.
- Wear earplugs—not the kind that swimmer's use, but a good pair you get from an ear doctor.

CAUTION

If the noise level in your job is loud enough to hurt your ears, it is already damaging your hearing.

Uncomfortable Office Furniture

When you're already staggering under a pile of reports, your stress will be compounded if your desk, computer angle, chair, or lighting isn't first-rate. Your own posture is also important. Sitting—especially slouching—puts continuous pressure on lower-back muscles and disks, while looking up and down from computers can strain the upper back.

You may not be able to get your boss to cough up a big-ticket item such as a new desk, but you may want to think about buying your own ergonomic chair if your boss won't spring for it.

It's important to take the time to arrange your working environment so you're comfortable. Think about how much time you spend in your office chair. Are you comfortable in it?

- Do you ever go home with a tired, aching back?
- Do the tendons in your arm hurt after using a computer all day?
- Does your spine feel stiff or uncomfortable?
- Does your head ache after you leave the office?

These are all signs of poorly fitting office furniture. Your backache may be caused by either a poorly designed chair or by the fact that you're not sitting in it correctly.

Desk and Chair Comfort

A good chair is essential to stress-free office work. If you decide to buy your own, look for a chair that gives you adjustments for height, back, and seat tilt. If possible, it's nice to find one with height-adjustable arms that swing out of the way. Now that you have a good chair, make sure that the chair-desk combination is set up correctly:

- Set your seat height so your feet are flat on the floor.
- There should be no undue pressure on the underside of your thighs near the knees.
- Your knees should not slope too much.
- Your desk should be a comfortable height for work. If you're short, this may be impossible—raise the seat height and use a footrest.

- Adjust the chair backrest height so your buttocks fit into the space between the backrest and the seat pan. The backrest should support the hollow of your back; adjust its tilt as necessary.
- If you spend a lot of time leaning back while you use a computer, experiment with a chair with a taller backrest.
- The seat should be big enough so you can change your position often and firm enough to support your weight through the buttocks, not the thighs.

Computer Comfort

One of the prime sources for work stress involves the computer—its screen, proper placement of the keyboard, and so on. Don't make the common mistake of putting the monitor, keyboard, or both off to one side on a desk. If you type more than a few minutes a day, the keyboard and monitor should be placed directly in front of your normal sitting position. To make sure you're getting the most comfort from your computer:

- Place your keyboard directly in front of you at seated elbow height.
- A keyboard that's too high causes twisting, awkward posture, and uneven body loads. Too-high or too-low placement also contributes to poor shoulder posture.
- A slight backward tilt of the keyboard to level the keys helps wrist posture while typing. The keyboard's surface should be as flat as possible.
- The mouse should be as close to the keyboard as possible and at the same height.
- Avoid placing the keyboard in a tray without enough room for the mouse.
- Place the screen between 18 and 30 inches from your eyes (about an arm's length).
- The top of your monitor should be at eye level, because you'll be most comfortable looking straight ahead but slightly downward. (That's why reading lenses in bifocal glasses are placed just below the horizontal plane.)

Comfort While Keyboarding

- Black characters against a light-gray background are the easiest on the eyes for long periods of time. Adjust brightness and contrast for the brightest screen without blurring.
- Often-used items should be within reach from your keyboarding position. A document holder should be at the same height and distance as the screen, so your eyes don't need to change focus.
- If you use a telephone often, use a headset to avoid bending your neck while typing.
- Change your sitting position every 15 minutes; take an active break every half hour, especially if you're typing more than two or three hours a day.
- Blink often while typing. (Keyboarders tend not to blink for long periods, which can dry out your eyes.)

CAUTION

Be sure to look away from the screen at least every 20 minutes and focus on something more than 20 feet away.

STEP BY STEP

Stress-Free Computer Posture

- *Relax your shoulders.*
- *Let your elbows swing free.*
- *Keep your wrists, knuckles, and top of forearm straight.*
- *Don't use commercial wrist pads; type from a "floating wrist" position.*
- *Drop your wrists to the wristpad for rest periods only.*
- *Use the lightest possible finger pressure while typing.*
- *Pull your chin in to look down; don't flop your head forward.*
- *Keep the hollow in the base of your spine.*
- *Lean back in your chair.*
- *Don't slouch or slump forward.*
- *Alter your posture from time to time.*
- *Every 20 minutes, get up and bend your spine backward.*

DEFINITION

ergonomics: *The science of adjusting your work environment to fit your body and make it comfortable.*

STEP BY STEP

Keyboard Exercise Minibreaks

Shoulder Blade Squeeze

1. *Raise your forearms and point your hands to the ceiling.*
2. *Push your arms back and squeeze your shoulder blades together.*
3. *Hold for 5 seconds.*
4. *Repeat three times.*

Eye Palming

1. *Place your elbows on your desk.*
2. *Cup your hands.*
3. *Close your eyes.*
4. *Place your eyelids gently onto your palms.*
5. *Hold position for one minute while breathing deeply and slowly.*
6. *Uncover eyes slowly.*

Arm and Shoulder Shake

1. *Drop your hands to your sides.*
2. *Shake your relaxed hands, arms, and shoulders gently for at least 5 seconds.*
3. *Repeat three times.*

Pianist's Finger Spread

1. *Place your arms straight in front of you.*
2. *Spread your fingers as far as possible for at least 5 seconds.*
3. *Repeat five times.*
4. *You can combine this with the forearm stretch by having the backs of your hands touch and then turning them so palms face ceiling.*

HABITS & STRATEGIES

If you wear glasses, tell your eye doctor about your monitor use and its distance from your eyes. You may need lenses adjusted for the distance of your computer monitor.

DEFINITION

repetitive strain injury: *An injury associated with any repetitive activity such as computer use.*

carpal tunnel syndrome: *A specific, severe, and debilitating form of repetitive strain injury that involves squeezing of the nerve to the hand by swollen tendons. It is a common result of excessive typing.*

The level of stress hormones in working mothers rises each morning and stays high until bedtime. Number of children at home makes no difference in stress levels. Men, however, experience a drop in stress levels when they come home from work.

Lighting

If you can't see what you're typing, you're bound to strain your eyes and your whole body in an attempt to decipher the letters on a monitor. The best way to avoid stress from poor lighting is to have a combination of fluorescent and incandescent light. What you want to do is reduce glare and reflection from your computer screen, nearby glass, or shiny surfaces.

If your office has windows, use blinds, shades, or drapes to control the amount of daylight in the room. Try putting the computer so the side of the display faces the windows; this can help minimize glare. Avoid bright light sources in your field of vision.

If you smoke while typing, you'll need to clean your screen often, because the smoke and water vapor combine to cloud up the surface of the computer.

Sleepless in Seattle

An appalling number of workers report that job stress is so intense they have trouble falling asleep at night. When you have trouble getting enough sleep at night, you tend to have a host of problems the next day: poor concentration and trouble making decisions, solving problems, and handling people. These

STEP BY STEP

Tired-eye Soother

If your eyes are irritated and tired from overwork and computer stress, try this 10-minute routine to relax and soothe your eyes:

- *Bend over a sink and splash your eyes several times with cold water.*
- *Place a hot washcloth over your closed eyelids, pressing your eyes gently with fingertips.*
- *Alternate the cold water splash and the hot washcloth several times.*
- *End with the cold water splash.*
- *Rub an ice cube around each eye several times.*
- *Pat your eyes dry with a soft towel.*
- *If you can, lie down with your feet slightly elevated; place a chilled cucumber or cool, wet tea bag over each closed eye.*

Half of all American workers say they sometimes have problems falling asleep at night because of job stress. And two-thirds of these people say their lack of sleep hurts their job performance.

problems cause more stress, which means that the next night it's even harder to fall asleep—and so the cycle continues.

Don't use sleeping pills. If you're struggling with stress-related insomnia, try not to use sleeping pills. They do help you fall asleep, but they can interrupt the sleep cycle so you don't get a restful night's sleep. If your sleeping problems are so bad that you feel you need more than an occasional sleeping pill, see your doctor.

The solution is to try to relieve stress so you can sleep:

- Exercise a few hours before bedtime.
- Eat lightly and don't drink caffeinated beverages.
- Take a warm bath right before bedtime.
- Listen to soothing music in bed.
- Don't sleep late on weekends; that will only start the insomnia problem over again on Sunday night.

CAUTION

Drink plenty of water at work. The first symptom of dehydration is fatigue, not thirst!

STEP BY STEP

Antistress Work Diet

For a pick-me-up at work and to prevent midmorning and midafternoon blood sugar drops, try the following:

- *Eat complex carbohydrates.*
- *Reduce intake of sweets.*
- *Restrict yourself to only one or two cups of coffee a day.*
- *Drink lots of water.*
- *Eat healthy snacks.*

Commuting Stress

Rush-hour logjams. Drive-by shootings. Car hijackings. Car pools. Smog alerts. Filthy subways, crowded buses, unreliable mass transit. Just getting to the job can be a major undertaking.

If you can't avoid a long commute, here are some tips to reduce your reaction to that vein-popping frustration of stop-and-go travel:

- Listen to gentle, relaxing music.
- Leave 30 minutes early to avoid rush hour. If your employer doesn't offer flexible work hours, see if you can start such a program.
- Listen to books on tape or relaxation cassettes.
- Tune in to a lively talk show, or dial up public radio and learn something.
- Exercise before leaving for work or when you return home so you'll be more relaxed.
- Find less-hectic roads on which to travel.
- Do deep-breathing exercises (read more about this in Chapter 8).
- Don't weave in and out of lanes just to get a car or two ahead. Ultimately, that's more stressful than just sitting there.
- Learn a foreign language by listening to tapes as you sit.
- Take alternative routes and appreciate the scenery.

- Listen to the radio traffic reports before starting the commute so you know which routes to avoid; carry a map if you need to look for an alternative way.
- Take public transportation, which may at least spare you from having to drive in bumper-to-bumper traffic.

Stress-Free Business Travel

Traveling for business may sound like fun, but in fact it's usually very stressful. To get through it with the least amount of tension, try the following suggestions:

- Finish packing your bags two days before you have to leave.
- Make a to-do list and try to complete it two days before you leave.
- If your business calls for frequent travel, keep a bag packed with items you always use (shaving cream, toothpaste, hair dryer, razor) and clothing.
- Some frequent business flyers reduce stress by keeping a complete business wardrobe packed and ready to go.
- The day before you leave, make a list of those things you need to do immediately upon your return.

Stress Busters When Traveling Across Time Zones

- *Three nights before you leave, go to bed an hour earlier for each time zone you'll cross heading east; do the opposite if you're going west.*
- *Limit caffeine (coffee, tea, chocolate, colas).*
- *Don't use sleeping pills.*
- *Drink plenty of water and juice.*
- *Don't overindulge in alcohol.*
- *When you arrive, spend as much time as possible outdoors in daylight. Spend at least one hour outdoors for every time zone you cross.*
- *Don't nap. Try to stay up during the day and go to bed in the evening.*

- Get plenty of sleep; avoid foods containing caffeine.
- Schedule an "adjustment day" to give you at least one full day to recuperate between the time you get home and when you have to go back to work.

What's Next?

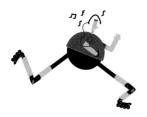

In Chapter 6, you'll learn about how to manage stress on the home front. Keep reading!

6

Stress Management at Home

- Identify your stress
- Conquer your stress
- Clean out clutter
- Time for yourself
- Stress-free finances
- Stress-free childrearing
- Simplify your life

FAST FORWARD

Handling Household Jobs ➤ *p. 87*

Two-career families report enormous stress over dividing at-home job responsibilities, especially between spouses. You and your partner need to pinpoint areas of contention around the home. Then plan to solve those problems.

1. Divide jobs evenly.
2. Be fair and flexible.
3. Don't complain about your spouse's performance.
4. Make a job jar.
5. Assign jobs or rooms and switch weekly.
6. If all else fails, hire help.

Do Away with Clutter ➤ *p. 88*

- Identify excess.
- Be heartless—get rid of anything expendable.
- Put out only half your treasures; store the other half and then rotate them.

Time-Out ➤ *p. 89*

Take time out for yourself to de-stress.

- Tell your family what you need.
- Make sure your partner also has some time off.
- Take turns sleeping in on the weekends.
- Find a private haven at home.

Stress-Free Kids ➤ *p. 90*

Raising kids today can be very stressful. Here are some tips:

- Carpool whenever possible.
- Share the volunteer duties with your spouse.
- Hire help with the kids.
- Find a part-time housekeeper/nanny. If you can't afford one, consider "kidpooling."

Daily Routines ➤ *p. 91*

Mornings are some of the worst time for stress, so it's a good idea to set up a morning and evening routine:

- Get up early.
- Set out clothes the night before.
- Set out breakfast the night before.
- Assemble backpacks and briefcases, homework, papers, show-and-tell, money, and permissions the night before.

Household Cleanup ➤ *p. 91*

You need a system if you're going to avoid stress at home when it comes to cleaning.

- Launder once a week only. Kids can take care of their own clothes.
- Assign kids to keep toys picked up and out of public areas.
- Use a portable cleaner regularly instead of vacuum.

Stress-Free Finances ➤ *p. 92*

- Analyze where your money is going.
- Budget—but leave some space for frivolity.
- Save something, anything, no matter how small.
- It's never too late to start saving.
- Pay off debt faster and you'll save big.

Simplify ➤ *p. 94*

- Hire help.
- Do one thing at a time.
- Screen your calls.
- Accomplish one small job a day.
- Bank electronically.
- Rely on the library.
- Don't be a clean freak.
- Simplify your social life.

In the halcyon days of the 1950s, before MTV, microwaves, and digital computers, a man's home was his castle and a woman spent her days in pearls and pumps happily vacuuming the rumpus room. Today, men and women compete head-to-head in a working world buffeted by downsizing and layoffs, and nobody has the time to vacuum anymore. It all seemed much simpler then. In today's world, we've got to share the responsibility for driving the kids to gymnastics, making the lasagna, and cleaning out the lint trap in the dryer. It isn't very surprising that polls are now reporting people feel more relaxed on the job than at home.

Work is the place where you can be creative and appreciated, where you get to do different and challenging things every day. You can spend happy minutes lolling around in front of the water cooler discussing last night's episode of the *X-Files*. Sometimes, you can even get away with closing the door to your office and doing the *New York Times* crossword puzzle.

Home is just a place that needs to be washed, waxed, and disinfected, week in and week out. Who's got time to throw together lobster Newburg, scrub the bathroom faucets, or help the kids concoct a map of Italy out of macaroni?

Busy People's Guide to the rescue! In this chapter, you'll learn how to winnow the necessary jobs from the chaff, pick up some strategies for managing this sort of stress, and get some help to put it all in perspective—and still have time left over to make that lobster Newburg.

Household Jobs

One of the most stressful aspects of at-home stress is doling out the job responsibilities in a two-career family. In your grandparents' generation, men were brought up to perform those once-in-a-while household jobs like toting the garbage. Women inherited all the little household tasks that need to be done every day, over and over. It might have been annoying, but at least they got to watch Loretta Young sweep down that staircase on afternoon TV while they scrubbed.

Now that everybody is at work and nobody has time for anything, couples report enormous stress over dividing up these at-home responsibilities. *How many times have you said . . .*

"She criticizes everything I do."

"He never does anything around the house."

"She never checks the oil and she always leaves the gas tank empty."

"How come he can run a marketing division but he doesn't know you don't put wool in a hot dryer?"

If you've ever heard any of these complaints—or found yourself saying them—it's time to stop and figure out what you can do about it. Take our word for it, the stress is only going to get worse.

Identifying Household Stress

- If you made a list of what you and your spouse do around the house, would the job distribution be about equal?
- If you stopped doing the laundry or changing the beds, would your spouse pick up the slack without comment?
- Do you and your spouse accept uncritically how well the other performs household tasks?
- If one of you wanted to hire a cleaning person, would the other agree?
- If one of you wanted to hire a lawn-care professional, would the other agree?
- If your child gets sick, do you share responsibility for staying home from work to provide nursing care?

If you answered no to more than one of these questions, odds are good that there are some stressful feelings at your house over job responsibilities. Here's what you can do about it:

Conquering Household Stress

1. First you need to get everybody on the same page. Write down a list of jobs you each perform. If the list is unequal, try dividing the responsibilities more evenly. Put some effort into deciding which jobs take more time or are done every day versus jobs that are done only once a week or month.

2. Aim for flexibility.

3. Don't complain about the way your spouse completes the job. Remember, you're not your spouse's parent—you're partners. Start acting like it. Remember, one of you isn't simply "helping out" with a job—it's an equal responsibility.

4. If you have trouble assigning jobs, make a job jar with necessary tasks written on pieces of paper. Select new jobs each week.

5. If that's too much like homework, assign jobs to each and switch weekly.

6. Assign rooms for every member of the family to clean. The following week, switch. Kids can get into this, too. You don't want your kids to grow up with gender-specific ideas about household jobs.

7. If all else fails, hire help: a cleaning person, lawn-care company, child care, pet sitter, and so on. Hiring help, if you can afford it, is always better than fighting over nonessentials.

"The homeliest tasks get beautiful if loving hands do them."
—Louisa May Alcott

Cut Down on Clutter

Ever wonder how the Shakers found the time to invent clothespins and round barns and still create beautiful furniture? For starters, you can bet they weren't wasting time dusting demitasse cups emblazoned with "Souvenir of the 1965 New York World's Fair." Shakers' homes were beacons of simplicity. Yours could be, too.

The power to organize and control the space in which you operate is imperative to a stress-free life.

If you find a messy, dusty home extremely stressful, take a page from the Shakers' hornbook. Do you really need all that *stuff?*

- *Identify excess.* Look around each room in your house with a critical eye. Which decorations and knickknacks do you really like, and which ones do you have around because you're too lazy to get rid of them?
- *Be heartless.* In every room, see if you can put away, give away, or sell at least half the dust-gathering items sitting on shelves and surfaces.
- *Be merciless.* If you haven't worn it in two years, odds are slim you ever will. Throw it out. Give it away. But don't clutter your life with tattered shirts and blue jeans that make you look like an advertisement for Jimmy Dean pork products.
- *Rotate.* If you're still left with too much kitsch, do what the Smithsonian people do. They don't have space for all their motley stuff either, so they stow most of it in the basement and display only a few pieces at a time. Then they shuffle those pieces off to storage and bring out something new.

Time-Out

It's not just for kids anymore! Taking a time-out from overwhelming social responsibilities is a healthy way to relieve the stress of overcommitment.

You know it's time for solitude if . . .

- The thought of having to go to another dinner party makes your stomach heave.
- You haven't had a weekend free for family time in more than a month.
- You can't finish one task at home without the phone ringing.
- You've spent more than three nights away from home in the last week.

Arranging Time Apart

- *Express yourself.* Tell your family honestly you need a brief time alone to recharge. Explain to young kids you still love them, but you need some privacy.

For many people, work now feels like home and home feels like work.

- *Trade off.* It's not fair for one member of the family to have solitude at the expense of others. Trade with your spouse so each of you can have a break during the weekend.
- *Sleep late on the weekend.* If both of you work outside the home, odds are that everyone has early mornings. One of you can sleep late on Saturdays and the other on Sundays. If church interferes with this schedule, alternate Saturday sleep-ins so that at least twice a month you have some time to rest on a weekend.
- *Find a private haven at home.* You may choose the bathtub, your small office, your bedroom. It's best if there's a door to guarantee solitude.

Stress-Free Kids

Raising kids has never been easy, but back in the days when moms automatically stayed home, it didn't create nearly the stress that it does today. How do you find time to drive everybody to their activities, volunteer at the school cafeteria, and sew Halloween costumes when you've got to be at your desk by 8:30 A.M.? What do you do when the kids are home sick or off for vacations?

Kid-Friendly Tips

Nothing is ever wasted if it makes a memory.

- *Carpooling is king.* While being able to drive your own kids everywhere is a terrific idea, in reality it may be impossible. Join together with other parents and carpool.
- *Share the volunteer duties.* While volunteering at your kids' school is important, you don't have to kill yourself, either. Alternate with your spouse; accept fewer requests for volunteer time.
- *Hire help.* Your mom may have had time to stitch 3,000 sequins on your Cinderella costume, but times are different now. Consider hiring a seamstress or buying a costume.
- *Home alone?* Hire a college student to stay with your kids after school. It's a good idea to have someone there when they get home.

Daily Routines

There's almost nothing as stressful as trying to get an entire family out the door to school and work in one piece and on time. When you don't have time to prepare the night before, you fall even further behind the next day. Result: you arrive at work exhausted, disheveled, and stressed out. No wonder people consider work a haven!

Here's how to set up a smooth morning routine:

More than 48 percent of Americans have begun to voluntarily simplify their lives in the last five years.

- *Rise early.* Set the alarm and get up an hour before you need to be out the door. This rule applies to everyone.
- *Have clothes laid out.* Get outfits together the night before. This way you will notice what needs to be ironed, what needs to be sewn, and what needs to be shredded for hamster bedding.
- *Prepare breakfast ahead.* Set the table the night before. Pour milk into a small kid-friendly pitcher and put dry cereal in bowls so small kids can prepare their own cereal in the morning.
- *Have briefcase ready to go.* Keep a folder or basket by the door for kids' papers, slips, and money that need to be taken that day. Pack backpacks and briefcases the night before and pile them by the door.

Household Cleanup

Your mother might have vacuumed every day and washed the woodwork once a week, but these days you need to accept the fact that you just don't have the time to compete with Martha Stewart.

More than 53 percent of American mothers with children under age 1 are currently holding down a job outside the home.

- *Laundry.* Wash once a week—and only what's dirty. Assign older kids' responsibility for their own clothes. Hand out one towel a week to each person.
- *Clutter.* If kids can't keep their toys picked up, require that toys stay in bedrooms or playrooms. Assign each person in the family their own room to clean each week.

- *Spot cleaning.* Invest in a handheld portable vacuum. Instead of dragging the big vacuum out every day, run the small cleaner to pick up crumbs and pet hair in between major vacuum days.

Carve Out a Niche

In a stressful world, it's important to have your own space to get away from the madding world. Only a few of us have our own private office at work where we can close the door and shut out the world. Even fewer have the luxury of a private office at home.

You may not be able to commandeer an entire room with a door that locks, but perhaps you can locate some little space at home that's all yours.

- *Find a place.* If you don't have room in your home for your own office, try blocking off areas with furniture, screens, or blinds.
- *Personalize.* Make whatever space you find your own by bringing in personal objects such as small plants or photos of people you love.
- *Be creative.* You may not have an entire room you can appropriate for your own, but what about a small closet in a little-used guest room? You can take off the doors, install a desk, and decorate.
- *Redecorate.* Perhaps you have some space in the basement or attic that you could turn into a getaway spot. What's important is that you feel you have a sanctuary.

Stress-Free Finances

You'd think that with both of you working, money would be the least of your worries, but that doesn't seem to be the case. Polls show that couples find one of the most stressful areas on the home front is dealing with money. There's never enough, and what there is usually causes disagreement about how it will be spent.

No one can live a stress-free life under the shadow of bankruptcy or homelessness. The first steps toward financial self-sufficiency are as follows:

The average American carries nine credit cards.

- *Analyze.* Figure out where your money is going. Write down every penny you spend over a week's time. That ought to shock you enough to get serious about your finances.

More than 60 percent of adult Americans don't have a will.

- *Budget.* That six-letter word doesn't have to be so painful if you allow yourself a small amount of money each week to waste. Psychologically speaking, if you force yourself to hoard every penny, you'll resent the plan so much that you'll likely sabotage your efforts. The key word here is *small.* Don't blow half your salary and expect to achieve financial independence.

- *Save something.* While it's nice to save the 15 percent weekly income the experts say you should, too many people figure if they can't save this much they won't bother to save anything. No amount is too small to start with. If you give up a daily cup of coffee at $1.25, that adds up to $6.25 a week, or $25 a month.

- *It's never too late.* You're 55 and you've never saved, so it's too late, right? Nope. Start today. Now. This second. Put that $1.25 in change in a jar and don't look back. In 20 years, you'll be glad you did.

- *Pay off debt faster.* You can pay off your credit card debt faster and save big if you add just a few extra dollars to your check each month. Credit card debt of $3900 at 18 percent interest will take you years to repay and cost more than $10,000 in interest if you make only the minimum payment each month. By adding just $10 a month to your payment, you'll pay off the debt in just six years and two months, and you'll save $7500 in interest.

HABITS & STRATEGIES

If you add just $25 a month to a 30-year fixed-rate 8 percent mortgage, you'll save $23,337 in interest over the life of the loan. If you can pay an extra $100 a month, you'll save $62,456!

Shhhhh

Simon and Garfunkel were on to something when they wrote their paean to silence. There's not enough of it anymore, and the constant din of technology in our homes can be stressfully deafening. At your house, how many of the following do you have?

- Videos
- CDs
- Stereo
- TV
- Microwave
- Coffee grinder
- Vacuum
- Computer games
- Electronic games
- Food processor
- Bread baker
- Electric ice cream maker

Now imagine if—as at most homes—only *half* these devices are whirring, jangling, and shrieking at the same time. Is it any wonder we're happier at work?

If there's too much noise in your house, pull the plugs. Set up quiet times for studying, thinking, or just talking to each other. Make sure the dinner hour is inviolable. Soft dinner music should be the only electrical sounds wafting over your dinner table.

Simplify

You spend your days racing to volunteer commitments, job, child care, and home. On the weekends you juggle parties, dinners out, chauffeuring the kids, paying bills, and doing chores.

It's probably easier for you to identify your stress than to get rid of it. Your husband throws his underwear behind the bathroom door. Your wife leaves the lights on. Mother-in-law drops in unexpectedly. The new baby has colic. Not much you can do about any of those. Instead, many people these days combat home stress by simplifying.

Eight Ways to Simplify Your Life

- *Hire help.* If it costs only $10 to reset the sleeves in a suit that doesn't fit and it would take you half a day to do a poor job, which choice makes the most sense?

- *Do one thing at a time.* You may think you're clever when you work on a report while talking on the phone and dealing with your kids, but odds are you're only building stress and not doing any of the jobs well.
- *Screen your calls.* A simple $20 answering machine can effectively screen out all those annoying telemarketer calls and people who want to chat when you don't have the time.
- *Do one small job a day.* Instead of having to call in the National Guard to hack through the mess over a weekend, parcel out the jobs in smaller bites. It can be overwhelming—and stressful—to contemplate a major job. Instead, set yourself one task. Clean out the laundry closet. When it's over, you're done.
- *Bank electronically.* Pay as many bills as possible electronically. Have your paycheck deposited automatically. You can even contribute to some mutual funds and other savings plans automatically. You'll avoid the stress of standing in line, finding postage, losing bills.
- *Rely on the library.* Take books and videos out of the library and you'll save space at home. Even better, read magazines there—you'll save money and avoid the piles of clutter. Xerox any articles you want to keep.
- *Don't be a clean freak.* There's no law that says your house needs to pass a health department inspection. Clean is one thing, but disinfected and hermetically sealed is unnecessary and stress-inducing.
- *Simplify your social life.* Instead of planning elaborate, expensive, and time-consuming gourmet meals for 25 people, invite a few friends over for a casual Sunday brunch or a bowl of hearty soup and "home-made" bread—from the bakery. What counts is the fellowship, not the glitz.

HABITS & STRATEGIES

No matter how busy you are, never miss an opportunity to tell your children you love them.

What's Next?

Now that you've got a handle on your stress in general, at work and at home, you'll learn some ways to relax and ease out of the stress you can't get rid of any other way!

Relax Your Stress Away

FAST FORWARD

How Does Relaxation Reduce Stress? ➤ *p. 100*

Learning how to relax can help rest your mind and calm your body. It's best to schedule a time to relax or meditate every day. While a regular relaxation session should take 20 or 30 minutes, it's possible to combine relaxation with other techniques so you can instantly relax during any stressful situation.

Relaxation: The First Steps ➤ *p. 101*

1. Close your eyes and start at the top of your body.
2. Concentrate on each muscle group, relaxing each one in turn.
3. *Alternative method:* Tense each muscle group first, then relax. Move on to the next set.
4. When you get to your toes, you should be completely relaxed.

Countdown Relaxation ➤ *p. 104*

1. First do a progressive relaxation of all muscles.
2. Count down slowly from 10 to 1, visualizing the numbers in front of you.
3. At the same time, imagine you are descending on an escalator or floating downward on a cloud.
4. When you get to the bottom, imagine you are in a lovely relaxing place.

Meditation ➤ *p. 104*

1. Relax your body.
2. As you breathe out, silently repeat a word or a phrase (such as *om* or *peace*).
3. Let any stray thoughts go calmly. Return to your word.
4. Continue for 10 or 15 minutes.

Visualization ➤ *p. 105*

If you have trouble meditating on "nothing," you may find it easier to use visualization to relax. Picture a calm, peaceful place in your mind. Allow yourself to wander around, taking in the sights, sounds, and smells. Give yourself a positive statement: "I feel calm" or "I feel peaceful." Try making the visualization proactive: "Whenever I'm in a stressful situation, I will react calmly and feel peaceful."

Self-Hypnosis ➤ *p. 107*

Self-hypnosis isn't a trick, it's just a very deep state of relaxation. Once deeply relaxed, you can give yourself suggestions on how to handle stress or other personal problems. You can also give yourself the suggestion to return to this state of deep relaxation at any time, using a trigger word such as *relax*.

Other Ways to Fight Stress ➤ *p. 109*

For alternative, brief methods to handle stress, try these:

- *Stroke a pet.* It is calming and will reduce blood pressure.
- *Take a hot bath.* Showers, baths, or hot tubs/saunas relieve tension and may boost positive brain chemicals.
- *Listen to music.* Soothing music can ease stress and lower blood pressure. Pick calming music to get the full benefits.
- *Have a laugh.* A humorous book or video can ease stress.

You don't need to sit on a mountaintop wearing a saffron robe and a wreath of flowers to learn to relax. Relaxation is the perfect exercise for busy people, because it doesn't take any elaborate preparations, it's easy to do, it's free, and it's completely portable. Relaxation training is a very important part of stress management. When you know how to relax your body, you'll automatically reduce the harmful effects of stress. And being able to stay calm in the face of stress can provide you with a real sense of self-control.

There are different approaches to relaxation training, and in this chapter you'll learn about the most important ones, from simple relaxation strategies to self-hypnosis and traditional meditation.

How Does Relaxation Reduce Stress?

When you relax or meditate, you focus your thoughts on something besides stressful thoughts for a period of time. This has the effect of resting your mind and channeling it away from stress-causing problems. As you relax or meditate, your body has time to recuperate, clearing away toxins that have built up during those stress-filled hours during the day. Withdrawing from problems and calming your mind can calm your body, blunting the adrenaline surge of stress.

When you do relaxation exercises or mediate, here's what happens to your body:

- Breathing slows.
- Blood pressure drops.

Put a piece of colored tape on your watch and on your clock at work. Now each time you glance up to see what time it is—a guaranteed stress builder—you'll see the reminder to relax. Say the word relaaaax *to yourself and feel your tension dissipate!*

- Muscles relax.
- Anxiety lessens.
- Stressful thoughts disappear.
- Irritability eases.
- Stress headaches fade away.
- Clear thinking improves.
- Focus and concentration improve.

When to Use It

Many people find it helpful to schedule relaxation or meditation into every day, a time set aside specifically to reduce stress. That may seem daunting to really busy people—reserving time every day to . . . *do nothing?*

Ideally, you'll notice significantly fewer hassles with stress if you can manage to do this every day. Some people like to start off the day with a meditation or relaxation period of about 20 minutes; others like to use it to unwind after a rough day. Then there are those superbusy people with extremely stress-filled jobs who find they perform better when using part of their lunch hour to meditate.

If you're not the sort of person who likes to schedule things like this, consider turning to relaxation or meditation on an as-needed basis. The techniques can be especially useful in the following scenarios:

- You find yourself worrying about problems.
- You've been constantly on the go and you feel exhausted.
- You've been under lots of short-term stress and you can feel adrenaline surging through your body.

Relaxation: The First Steps

First things first. Before you can begin to meditate, you need to be able to relax your body. That's a trick in itself when you're feeling stressed. Most busy people go about trying to relax at the same pace they do everything else. *Stop!* Don't worry about doing it right. Don't worry about how much time it's taking. Don't worry about whether or not just sitting there is productive.

If you need a reason—and busy people often do—consider this: When you relax, your body and mind slow down. Time spent away from stress will help you tackle difficult situations with renewed energy and a reenergized outlook.

You'll probably be surprised at how much tension you find in your muscles. Until you relax them, you may not have realized how tight some of those muscles were. No wonder so many busy people feel as taut as a bowstring after a whole day of this!

Here's how to begin:

1. Find a position that feels comfortable, either sitting or lying down.

2. Close your eyes.

3. Relax your arms with hands slightly folded on your lap.

4. Begin taking slow, deep breaths.

5. Breath rhythmically from the abdomen, not the chest.

6. As you say the word *relax* silently to yourself, focus on the muscles at the top of the head and consciously relax them.

7. When you feel the top of your head seem to relax, move down to the eye area. Keep repeating *relax* as you consciously focus on each muscle group. Don't move on until you can feel that area relax.

8. Move on to the sinus area of your face, and *relax*.

9. Move to the muscles of your ears and the back of your neck. This is the seat of quite a lot of tension, so spend some time here. Don't move on until you can actually feel those muscles loosen.

10. Move all the way down to your toes, relaxing each section of your body.

For more detailed information about breathing, see Chapter 8.

This is just one very effective way of relaxing your muscles. If you're extremely busy, you could stop there and still be ahead of the game. If you're enjoying this feeling, and you'd like to know more, you could take yourself to a deeper state of relaxation with meditation or self-hypnosis, which we'll discuss later in this chapter.

There are different ways to relax, of course. If you don't feel that simply focusing on a muscle and *willing* it to relax will get the job done, an alternative method follows.

Some people have trouble visualizing white light. If you do, imagine white light as a thick mist or fog.

Progressive Muscle Relaxation (PMR)

1. Close your eyes and sit or lie down comfortably.

2. Relax your arms with hands slightly folded on your lap.

3. Begin taking slow, deep breaths.

4. Breath rhythmically from the abdomen, not the chest. You should be able to see your stomach pushing out.

5. Start at the muscles at the back of your head and neck. Firmly tense and tighten just those muscles. Hold for 5 seconds, and then relax those muscles.

6. It is important to keep the rest of your body relaxed while you're tensing one group of muscles (this isn't as easy as it sounds!).

7. As you relax the muscles, concentrate and focus on the tension leaving. Visualize the muscle becoming relaxed.

8. If you have trouble tensing and relaxing, practice first with your fist. Clench it tightly, and then relax. This is what you should be aiming for with each muscle group.

9. As you relax the muscles, imagine white light and warm energy filling the area.

10. Work your way down your body, tensing and relaxing one muscle group at a time. Concentrate on keeping the rest of your body relaxed.

The muscles of your head, face, neck, and shoulders are tension hot spots. Make sure these areas have relaxed fully before moving on to other parts of your body.

CAUTION

If you have an injury or a weak muscle group, use caution when tensing that area. You might want to skip it altogether.

HABITS & STRATEGIES

Link PMR to a key word (like relax). Because you've associated the key word with the feeling of relaxation, you'll be able to instantly recall this feeling during a moment of stress by silently repeating the key word to yourself.

Countdown Relaxation

The preceding methods are good ways to start off learning how to relax. Now you're ready to work toward deeper relaxation states. This will help you become deeply relaxed at will—which comes in handy during a busy, stressful day.

Handling tension is all about self-control. Counting is a good way to achieve this. Here's how to start:

1. Close your eyes and go through one of the previously listed relaxation exercises.

2. When you've relaxed your muscles, start counting backward slowly from 10 to 1.

3. As you count, visualize yourself *descending*—either riding on a slowly moving escalator, walking down stairs, or floating downward on a cloud.

4. As you descend, visualize each number as you say it.

5. Every few numbers, say to yourself, "I'm becoming more relaxed. When I get to zero, I will be totally relaxed."

6. Go at your own pace. Descend only as fast you can comfortably feel yourself relax.

7. When you get to the bottom, imagine a peaceful, beautiful scene. It should be a place you *want* to get to!

With practice, you should be able to reduce the time of the number countdown, perhaps beginning with five and counting to zero. Some people have been able to pare it down to just three numbers.

Meditation

Now that you've learned how to enter a state of light relaxation, you can experiment with a deeper relaxed state of meditation. Eastern religions have practiced meditation for centuries, which should be some indication that it really does work. In fact, meditating can have all the benefits of popping a Valium, without the side effects.

1. Follow the previously listed steps to relax your body.

2. Focus on your breathing. As you breathe out, silently repeat a word or a phrase (such as *om* or *peace*).

3. When thoughts pop into your head, calmly let them go. Return to your word.

4. Continue for 10 or 15 minutes at first; you may wish to extend your mediation as you become more experienced.

After several weeks of practice, most people say they feel not only more relaxed after meditating, but more likely to stay calm in response to stress.

However, meditation doesn't work for everybody. Some folks get so relaxed they simply drift off into sleep. Others tie themselves into knots because they can't master the art of thinking about nothing. If this is your problem, you might have more success with visualizing—this is still calming, but instead of focusing on emptying your mind, you present your mind with a relaxing picture or image.

Visualization

Visualization is a more active procedure than meditation. For type A folks and others who live in a stressful world, it may be easier to accomplish, since you are actually *doing* something with your mind.

Basically, visualization involves relaxing yourself and then imagining a calming scene. We all know how some environments can be relaxing and others intensely stressful. The principle behind visualization and imagery is that you can use your mind to re-create a relaxing place. The more intensely you call up the scene in your mind, the stronger and more realistic the experience will be. In *active visualization* you can give yourself suggestions, called *affirmations,* while you're in the scene.

1. Go through a total-body relaxation as previously discussed.

2. When you have fully relaxed, with eyes remaining closed, imagine a calm, beautiful scene in full detail. You can pick a place that you've already visited or make one up in your mind. This may take practice; some people are gifted visualizers, and others find this more difficult.

3. Don't merely visualize a picture. Listen to the wind blow. Smell the scent of new-mown hay. Feel the spray of the surf.

4. Still with your eyes closed and while you're in the scene, give yourself a positive affirmation: "I feel peaceful" or "I feel completely relaxed in every social situation."

5. Keep the affirmations *positive.* Don't say, "I want to stop feeling miserable and stressed." Instead say, "I will feel pleasantly relaxed and calm in every situation."

6. At the end of the visualization, tell yourself "When I open my eyes, I will feel calm, peaceful, and completely refreshed." Then open your eyes, and prepare to be amazed!

Visualizations can be used to de-stress after a busy day at work. They also can be used to prepare yourself for stress. In this case, instead of visualizing an imaginary scene, you'd preview the upcoming stressful situation, watching yourself act confidently and calmly. The more chances you have to preview such a situation, the more likely you'll be able to sail through it unscathed—just the way you imagine it.

If you're having a really hard time with stress, try these tips:

- Visualize yourself in the middle of a relaxing scene and picture stress actually flowing out of your body.
- Imagine your stress and everyday concerns being folded away and padlocked into a chest.
- Picture your worries, one by one, and imagine that you are taking each one and throwing it into a wastebasket beside you.

How Can a Picture in Your Mind Have Power?

Visualization works because your sense organs convert signals from your environment into nerve impulses that feed into the areas of the brain that interpret the environment. When you visualize, you are creating a similar set of nerve impulses that feed into those same areas. Because your brain can't tell the difference between what is real and what is actively imagined, this type of active visualization can truly make a difference in the way you deal with everyday situations. It's a trick professional athletes and top business executives use regularly to boost their performance. You can do the same thing.

Self-Hypnosis

No, we're not going to have you barking like a dog or eating a raw potato. Entertainers have gotten a lot of mileage out of cloaking hypnosis with a lot of mystery, magic, and mayhem. In fact, hypnosis is simply a state of mind where you are very relaxed and focusing your attention on suggestions. You can't be made to do something you wouldn't normally do.

Self-hypnosis is really a deeper form of active visualization with affirmations, where you direct your unconscious mind to reduce stress and induce relaxation. The beauty of self-hypnosis is that you don't have to go anywhere and you don't need to have a hypnotist involved—you can do it yourself, anywhere, anytime. With practice, it doesn't take much longer than a few minutes.

Before you enter this hypnotic state, it's a good idea to figure out what suggestions you want to give yourself when you are fully relaxed. You can use this to reinforce confidence, give yourself antistress messages, and so on.

Here's how to induce hypnosis yourself:

1. Relax yourself using the previously discussed methods.

2. Imagine waves of relaxation running down your body, washing away stress.

3. Time the waves to match your slowed breathing.

4. Now use suggestion to deepen this state of relaxation. It's nothing magical; just say to yourself, "I am feeling relaxed and comfortable. With every breath, I am becoming even more relaxed."

5. Speak the words in your mind slowly and softly.

6. Once you are completely relaxed, you can give yourself the suggestion that when you repeat a trigger word, you will relax and return to this

To test the depth of your relaxed state, command your pointer finger to rise, but don't consciously move the finger yourself. If you are indeed in a deep state of relaxation, your finger should rise without a conscious effort on your part. It may take a few tries in the beginning to achieve this state.

state of deep relaxation. Then you can use the trigger word almost anywhere, even at work in the middle of the day, to help cope with stress.

7. When you are finished, give yourself the suggestion that, on the count of three, you will awaken completely refreshed, relaxed, and energized.

HABITS & STRATEGIES

Try making your own self-hypnosis tape. With soothing background music, record your voice counting backward from 10 to 1. Give yourself relaxation suggestions and a few affirmations.

One-Minute Relaxation Technique

All of these relaxation techniques we've just discussed work very well, provided you have about 20 minutes to spend on them. A self-hypnotic suggestion works well if you've thought of it beforehand—but some people just aren't good at self-hypnosis.

When you're sitting outside the boss's office awaiting your performance review, or you're clutching your notes while waiting to give a speech to 250 restless salespeople, who's got 20 minutes to spend relaxing? For those moments when you just don't have much time, here's a guaranteed, on-the-spot stress reducer. As you feel yourself begin to get annoyed or tense, do the following:

1. Think "happy." Pull your lips into a smile and visualize your face creasing in happiness. Your mouth is smiling; your eyes are dancing. Say to yourself, "I'm just fine." When you think happy, it's hard to be stressed.

2. If thinking happy is too hard, fill yourself with love. Imagine someone you love and allow yourself to fully experience how much you love that person. Fill your body with love. It's a fact: you can't experience strong emotions like love and fear at the same time.

3. To help induce calmness, take a long, slow breath. Breathe the tension in and out. Feel calmness filling your lungs. Exhale and smile.

Other Ways to Relax

Any quiet pursuit, such as reading or spending time on a hobby, are moderately effective in helping you relax. But to reach a deeper state of relaxation—which is most helpful in reducing stress—try one of the following alternatives.

Listen to Music

Scientists have found that listening to music can reduce stress, slow your heart rate, and lower your blood pressure. To get the most benefit, it's probably best to choose Vivaldi over Metallica. Slow music is more soothing than fast; strings and woodwinds are more soothing than trumpets or discordant electric sounds; instrumentals are better than trying to follow the words to a song. To get the full benefit of stress-busting music:

1. First, pick music to match your mood—perhaps something along the lines of "Take This Job and Shove It."

2. Gradually change the music to reflect the mood you want to attain: Steven Halpern's "Dawn," Paul Winter's "Common Ground." Many New Age recordings have a smooth, relaxing flow. Or try a selection of environmental music—summer rain, woods noises, wind and surf with seagulls.

Soak Away Stress

Many people swear by a hot shower, bath, sauna, or hot tub to steam away their stress. If you live in a noisy household, the bathroom may be the only place you can be assured of 20 minutes of privacy.

The heat also eases tense muscles—if you arrive home with a tension headache, you can often find relief by standing under a hot shower. Some experts believe the hot steamy water also triggers the release of brain chemicals that produce a sense of well-being while lowering the level of stress hormones. Finally, a

Massage therapists offer a wide variety of techniques depending on your needs and their specialties, including hot and cold packs, heat lamps, and remedial exercise recommendations.

hot bath before bed appears to result in deeper, more restful sleep—another good way to ward off stress.

For increased benefit, add basil, bergamot, cedarwood, chamomile, geranium, lavender, rose, sage, or sandalwood to the bathwater.

Pet Pleasures

There's nothing like coming home to a loving pet to help you forget a stressful day. Scientists say there's a real health benefit in petting a dog or cat. Stroking an animal reduces blood pressure and eases stress—in both the human *and* the pet. Even the presence of a dog in the room seems to relax folks.

Of course, for some people, owning a dog or cat in the first place could create its own stress. If you're not a pet lover, consider getting a couple of goldfish. Studies also show that simply watching a tankful of fish cavorting through the seaweed is relaxing and reduces stress. Added benefit: fish don't throw up, track kitty litter through the house, or annoy the neighbors.

Have a Laugh

A good belly laugh can work wonders on your heart rate, blood pressure, and muscle tension and thus diffuse stressful situations. In ways similar to aerobic exercise, scientists have found that when you laugh, your blood pressure, heart rate, and muscle tension rise briefly. Then your blood pressure actually *drops* below pre-chortle levels. Presto! You're more relaxed.

This hasn't been lost on hospitals and nursing homes, which provide humor magazines and comics for their patients. You can do the same. Stock up on humorous tapes, videos of funny shows, book collections of humor. Reach for one of these when you're feeling totally stressed out.

Massage

If you're in the mood for sheer pampering, consider a therapeutic massage—one of the best ways to combat stress. Massage can dramatically reverse the damaging physiological effects of stress in the following ways:

- Lowers heart rate and blood pressure
- Improves circulation
- Raises skin temperature

Laughing for 20 seconds is equivalent to three minutes of rigorous rowing— without the calluses!

- Heightens sense of well-being
- Reduces anxiety level

During the massage, your tight muscles relax and the pain that comes with chronic tension dissolves. As your circulation gets a boost, your muscles will receive more oxygen and nutrients. Massage also stimulates more of those terrific endorphins.

What's Next?

By now you should be so relaxed you're almost asleep. Hold that thought! In the next chapter, you'll learn about breathing and stretching, and how these techniques can help you achieve even deeper levels of relaxation, whether used alone or in combination with the methods you learned in this chapter.

8

Breathing and Stretching Away Stress

INCLUDES

- Health benefits of breathing
- Anxiety breathing
- Deep breathing
- Stress-buster breathing techniques
- When to deep-breathe
- When and how to stretch
- Neck stretch
- Shoulder stretches
- Spinal stretches

FAST FORWARD

Breathing and Stress ➤ *p. 117*

Most of the time we all breathe incorrectly—taking shallow breaths instead of deep breaths. Deep breathing is essential for health and easing stress and is the single most effective way you can combat anxiety.

Anxiety Breathing ➤ *p. 118*

Most people take shallow "chest" breaths when they are stressed. Only the top of your lungs fill with air, which deprives your brain of oxygen. This triggers an increase in stress hormones, which increases your stress. When you feel constricted, lightheaded, or anxious under stress, you've been shallow-breathing.

Deep Breathing ➤ *p. 120*

Deep breathing is a very effective method of relaxation that includes everything from simple deep breaths to Zen meditation. Deep breathing is an important part of progressive muscle relaxation, relaxation imagery, and meditation. It boosts oxygen exchange, lowers heart rate and blood pressure, distracts you, and boosts your sense of control.

Stress-Buster Breathing ➤ *p. 120*

1. Sit up with your back straight.
2. Inhale deeply through the nose without forcing. Let your abdomen expand. Imagine air filling your abdomen.
3. In one continuous breath, fully expand chest and lungs.
4. Exhale slowly through your nose. Breathing out should take longer than breathing in.
5. Breathe for least a minute, keeping breathing deep and full.

When to Use Deep Breathing ➤ p. 123

You can use deep breathing when you feel tense or to *prevent* some stress symptoms. Deep breathing isn't magic; it's just the best stress reliever there is. You can practice your deep breathing at any time:

- Commuting to work
- Before a fine meal
- During sports activities
- Before a performance

Invigorating Breath ➤ p. 124

Other breathing techniques can invigorate you. This is helpful when you are so stressed that you feel depressed, burned out, or exhausted. Invigorating breathing exercises gives you the most oxygen in the shortest time.

1. Inhale for one count, using abdomen and lower ribs.
2. Inhale again while counting to 4, fully expanding rib cage and upper lungs.
3. Exhale orally for one count, relaxing throat and contracting rib cage.
4. Exhale again to 4, fully contracting the ribs and abdominals.

When and How to Stretch ➤ p. 125

Ideally, you should stretch every 30 minutes; if you can't, then stretch in the morning, at midmorning, lunch, midafternoon, and end of the day.

Neck Stretches ➤ p. 127

Periodically stretching your neck muscles can help ease tension.

1. Lift shoulders up to ears.
2. Rotate neck and head in large circles three times in each direction.

3. If tilting your head backward hurts, just draw imaginary circles with your nose.

Shoulder Stretches ➤ *p. 128*

To relieve shoulder tension:

1. Hold left arm just below the elbow with your right hand.
2. Pull your elbow toward your right shoulder.
3. Hold for three breaths; repeat on the other side.

Spinal Stretches ➤ *p. 129*

To relax your spine, lower back, and shoulders:

1. Lean forward in your chair, relaxing neck, shoulders, and back.
2. Rest chest on thighs.
3. Hang hands down.
4. Hold for count of three.
5. Curl your spine as you rise into a sitting position.

It seems obvious that if you're alive, you should be an expert on breathing, right? While all of us do the basic in-and-out breathing pretty well, most of us *don't* really breathe correctly. That is, we breathe from our chests—not from our diaphragms the way trained singers do. One of the reasons that lots of us don't breathe correctly is that we're so busy sucking in our stomach muscles to look fashionably thin that we inhibit the natural airflow to the lower portion of the lungs.

If you can control your breathing, you can control your heart rate and most other stress symptoms.

In this chapter, we're going to learn why we breathe the way we do and how we breathe when we're stressed. Then you'll learn how to breathe deeply, and we'll offer a range of exercises to help you learn to break the stress habit by breathing away tension.

Deep Breathing Is Healthy

One of the handy things about breathing is that we all breathe whether we think about it or not—that is, breathing is connected with both the involuntary (unconscious) and voluntary (conscious) nervous systems. Without thinking about it, you take air in and out; however, if you want to, you can control your breathing. This in turn can control your heart rate.

In fact, deep breathing is essential for your health *and* for stress management. In fact, of all the things you can do to alleviate anxiety, forming healthy breathing habits is likely to produce the most dramatic results. There is probably no single step that will so profoundly affect your body.

Anxiety Breathing

When the stress is building and you start to get anxious, you probably begin to take shallow "chest" breaths. This means that you're using your chest muscles to inhale instead of breathing from your diaphragm. Thus only the top part of your lungs fill with air.

So there you are, standing in an airport in Beirut and watching a hostage takeover. You're feeling mighty tense, and you start breathing shallowly. You've forgotten you've ever *had* a diaphragm, and you're breathing from your chest. Alarm bells go off in your brain as oxygen levels fall and stress chemicals pour into your blood. This sets up a vicious cycle: The more pronounced the shallow breathing, the more your brain pumps out stress hormones and the more anxious you become. You can't think straight. You feel even more tense. Your brain gets less oxygen than ever, and sends out even more stress hormones. . . .

To fully comprehend what's happening when you breathe shallowly, try this exercise:

- Lie down and contract your abdominal muscles as hard as you can.
- Notice your breathing; only your chest will rise as you inhale.
- Notice how your diaphragm remains in place and the air fills only the upper portion of your lungs.
- Relax your stomach muscles and breathe into your abdomen. See how your diaphragm moves down and the lower portion of your lungs fill up?
- Note how the two different types of breathing make you feel.

Yawning doesn't just mean you're bored; it's also a sign that you're not breathing correctly. It means your body is trying to take in more oxygen because you're not providing enough from normal breathing.

In fact, the way you breathe while sucking in your stomach is simply an exaggerated form of the improper way you probably breathe all the time.

When you're tense, do you ever feel constricted, lightheaded, or anxious? If you do, then you know you've been shallow breathing.

Too often, you'll forget to contract your abdominal muscles and completely exhale. This means you're left with old, used-up, stale air in your lower lungs. You need to learn to inhale and exhale correctly in order to take in the most oxygen and remove all of the carbon dioxide.

Track Your Diaphragm

Here's a way to really understand what we're talking about.

1. Lie down and take a deep, slow breath. Notice any chest movement.

2. Put your hand on your abdomen and allow your stomach to rise about an inch as you breathe in.

3. As you breathe out, notice that your abdomen falls about an inch. Your chest will rise slightly at the same time.

4. Become aware of your diaphragm moving down as you inhale and back up as you exhale. Remember, it is impossible to breathe from your abdomen if your diaphragm isn't moving down. And it's impossible to let your diaphragm move down if your stomach muscles are tight. Relax your stomach muscles.

HABITS & STRATEGIES

If you have trouble with deep breathing, try breathing in through your nose and out through your mouth.

Other Diaphragm Duties

When you don't breathe deeply and your diaphragm doesn't move correctly, it affects more than just your state of relaxation. The downward movement of your diaphragm massages and stimulates the liver, stomach, spleen, kidneys, adrenal glands, pancreas, and colon, which is crucial to their proper functioning. When you interfere with the movement of the diaphragm because you have lousy posture, tense abdominal muscles, and poor breathing habits, you interfere with the normal functioning of all of these organs. Everything comes crashing to a halt—or at least slows down to a snail's pace.

HABITS & STRATEGIES

See if you can catch yourself clenching your jaw, tensing your shoulders, knotting your hands, and so on. When you do, practice a few deep breaths and release the tension.

Deep Breathing

Deep breathing is a very effective method of relaxation that can include everything from simply taking a few deep breaths to yoga and Zen meditation. Breathing exercises go right along with the progressive muscle relaxation, relaxation imagery, and meditation discussed in Chapter 7.

How It Works

Deep breathing works not only by boosting your oxygen exchange, but by lowering your heart rate and blood pressure. It also distracts you from stressful situations and boosts your sense of control. When you know you can count on deep breathing to calm down, you regain a sense of control over your emotions, and the cycle of anxiety is broken.

Stress-Buster Breathing Techniques

There are a variety of ways you can practice stress-buster breathing—also known as *deep breathing* or *diaphragmatic breathing*. You can practice these exercises in any position, but while you're learning, it's probably best to practice lying down. (In situations where lying down on the floor might be a bit awkward—for example, in the middle of a boardroom—you can do the exercises sitting or standing.)

Stress-Buster Breathing #1

To increase the amount of oxygen you receive, do this exercise at least once a day for three weeks. This will help you learn the basic approach to switching from shallow to deep breathing. The more often you do it, the better the results:

1. Sit in a chair without armrests, feet flat and thighs parallel to the floor. Hold your back straight. Place your hands in your lap.

2. Inhale through your nose and breathe deeply, without forcing. Let your abdomen expand. Imagine air filling your abdomen.

3. In one continuous breath, imagine filling your chest and lungs with air. Feel your chest expand fully and your shoulders rise slightly

(keeping shoulders relaxed). Imagine the air expanding your abdomen and chest in all directions.

4. Exhale slowly through your nose. Breathing out should take longer than breathing in.

5. Do this breathing for at least a minute. Stay in a comfortable rhythm and don't strain yourself. Focus on keeping your breathing deep and full and your body relaxed.

DEFINITION

diaphragm: The dome-shaped muscle located at the bottom of the lungs that helps breathing by moving up and down.

Stress-Buster Breathing #2

1. As you inhale, count very slowly from one to four.

2. As you exhale, count slowly back down.

3. Do this for several breaths or as long as you need to.

Stress-Buster Breathing #3

1. As you inhale, begin to count down from 10, saying "ten."

2. Exhale.

3. As you inhale again, say "nine."

4. Keep counting down with each inhalation. If you start to feel light-headed, slow down.

5. When you get to "zero" you should be feeling much calmer! If not, start over at 10 and keep going.

Stress-Buster Breathing #4

Use any of the preceding methods, but as you breathe:

1. Pause after each time you inhale.

2. Pause again for a few seconds each time you exhale.

3. Do this for several breaths.

HABITS & STRATEGIES

To remember to practice your deep breathing, link the technique with an activity you do a couple of times a day: checking your watch, washing your hands, talking on the phone.

STEP BY STEP

Complete Breathing

This is another form of deep breathing that is very calming and will allow you to take in about 10 times more air than usual. This will help you increase your lung capacity and clear air passages, since it uses all parts of your lungs.

1. Place your palms at the sides of your ribs with your fingers around to the front.

2. Relax your abdominal muscles.

3. Inhale, expanding your rib cage sideways.

4. As you inhale, try to push your hands apart.

5. Now remove your hands and fill your lungs from bottom to top, taking two counts for the bottom, middle, and top of each lung section.

6. As you fill the upper part of your lungs, don't lift your shoulders. Feel your throat lightly constrict. (This lifts the ribs up and out to allow more air into the lungs.)

7. Exhale from the top to the bottom of your lungs, relaxing the throat.

8. As you exhale, squeeze the ribs from the sides, bringing the fingers of the two hands closer. Contract the rib cage area, and then contract the abdominal muscles completely.

9. Now inhale and try to push the hands apart.

STEP BY STEP

Rhythmic Breathing

This breathing exercise is mentally and physically calming. Hold each part of this breathing exercise for the same amount of time.

1. Inhale, filling the lower, then the middle, and finally the upper lungs, while counting to 10.

2. Hold your breath for 10 counts.

3. Relax your shoulders and your face. Maintain correct posture.

4. Exhale for 10 counts, emptying upper, middle, and lower lungs.

When to Use Deep Breathing

It's hard for most of us to breathe this way *all* the time. But this sort of deep breathing can come in handy anytime you are feeling mildly tense, anxious, or upset. In fact, you can even *prevent* some stress symptoms (butterfly flutters, dry mouth, heart pounding, and so on) by practicing deep breathing before a stressful situation.

You can also use these deep-breathing exercises in the face of severe stress. It's one of the techniques that experts teach patients who are struggling to conquer phobias—the most severe type of stress situation there is.

Deep breathing won't zap you into a state of nirvana. You won't be unconscious, semiconscious, or hypnotized. But what the technique will do is to restore your natural, healthy style of breathing. It can distract you from pain or anxiety, give you an energy boost, and sharpen your awareness. It's one of the best stress managers around.

You can practice your deep breathing at any time, not just when you're in the middle of a stressful crisis. Some suggestions follow.

Commuting to Work

You're sitting there in traffic staring at that BMW bumper in front of you. Here's a good time to practice deep breathing—you might even get through rush hour!

Before a Fine Meal

Taking a few well-timed deep breaths not only reduces anxiety, but reminds you to stop and appreciate the moment. Rather than just gulping down your meal, if you stop and take a few breaths you'll have an opportunity to savor what you are about to eat.

During Sports Activities

If you're playing a sport and you have a few seconds before taking a basketball shot, hitting your golf ball, serving in tennis, or beginning a horseback jumping round, take a few seconds and do some deep breathing. Athletes rely on many

Quick-fix Breathing

You're stuck in a tense situation. Your boss is shouting at you for making mistakes that aren't your fault during a presentation. You feel your face get red and your hands clench.

Stop. To release that tension and enable yourself to respond calmly, do as follows:

- *Take several slow, deep breaths.*
- *Return to normal breathing.*
- *Take several more slow, deep breaths.*

If the situation hasn't changed, give a mental shrug, drop your shoulders, and let your stress go.

techniques to center themselves, gather their resources, and focus. Deep breathing can help you do that, whether you're a professional athlete or a weekend hobbyist.

Before a Performance

Anytime we're called upon to perform, no matter how famous or skilled we may be, most of us have a nervous reaction. Taking some calming, deep breaths can help control those stress-related fears and prepare us to perform.

Invigorating Breath

Stress doesn't always show up as tension. You may be feeling extremely tired and dragged out. You may be depressed. You may be burned out. Certain deep-breathing exercises can be invigorating, pulling in fresh oxygen and snapping you out of the doldrums. This exercise gives you the most oxygen in the shortest period of time. It's a kind of breathing favored by long-distance runners because it tones all the breathing muscles.

When you're feeling down, do three of these:

1. Inhale for one count, using your abdomen and lower ribs.
2. Inhale again (without exhaling in between) while counting to 4, fully expanding the rib cage and upper lungs.

The foundation of any stress management program is proper breathing habits.

3. Exhale through the mouth for one count, relaxing the throat and contracting the rib cage area.

4. Exhale again to a count of 4, fully contracting the ribs and contracting the abdominals.

5. Completely squeeze out the carbon dioxide from the lower portion of the lungs.

Blow-Out Breath

Another good breathing technique that works well when you're dragging is the blow-out breath. This helps revitalize your body and clears your mind, strengthening the diaphragm and stomach muscles. It's also a good technique for anyone with asthma, which can often be worsened with stress.

CAUTION

Don't practice the blow-out breath if you have high or low blood pressure, an ear infection or an eye infection.

Explosive Breathing

Practice this breathing technique in sets of four to six breaths at a time, gradually building up to ten.

1. Lie on your back and put the soles of your feet close to your buttocks.

2. Close your eyes; focus your attention in the stomach area.

3. Breathe through your nose.

4. Exhale through your nose, strongly contracting your abdominal muscles.

5. Keep both inhalation and exhalation short and equal in length, pumping your lungs like a bellows.

Stretching Away Your Stress

There's a stack of briefs on your desk and another pile of reports to attack—all by 5 P.M. today. The later it gets, the tighter your muscles feel. But there's no time to go to the gym, no time to run down for a sandwich—not even time to dash over to the snack machines.

You know the longer you sit, the more tense your muscles will become. The blood will pool down around your toes. Your brain will get foggier by the minute. What you need are some easy stretching exercises that you can do right at your desk or on the job—something to break that tension habit.

CAUTION

Before beginning stretching exercises, consult your doctor if you have an illness or injury.

Muscles and Stress

You've got more than 400 different skeletal muscles packed away inside, and each one of them contracts when it's working and lengthens when it's relaxed. You feel energized after you exercise because of the increased flow of oxygen to your body. Stretching aids circulation and oxygen flow while reducing muscular tension.

Emotions like fear, anxiety, resentment, and anger cause muscles to contract. Stretching relaxes these tense muscles.

Identify Your Tension

We don't all react to external stress in the same way. Some people get upset stomachs, some get stiff necks, others have back spasms. To an enormous degree, however, our body expresses our state of mind. When you're slumped in your chair with your chin on your chest, it doesn't usually mean you're happy.

Trying to hide your emotions won't help, however. If you try to disguise your feelings, you create tension in your body from the attempt to suppress how you feel.

You can get rid of this emotional anxiety by stretching the tense area. That's why it's so important to know in which part of the body you hold your stress.

When and How to Stretch

If you combine the following exercises with the deep breathing you learned earlier in this chapter, you'll be on your way to a stress-free life. They work when you're already too tense, and they work to prevent stress in the first place.

Ideally, you should stop and stretch every 30 minutes. But that's just too often for some folks, so you could time your stretches to your break times—midmorning, lunch, midafternoon, end of the day.

Stretching at Your Computer or Desk

The best way to stay pain-free and flexible while you're slaving over a hot computer is to take stretching breaks every half hour or so. These miniroutines take only a few minutes, but they reduce stress, tension, and stiffness.

In fact, this concept has so much merit that some software manufacturers are working on reminder programs that will sound a chime every hour, flash an icon, and display a range of stretching exercises on the screen.

Neck Stretches

Anyone who has ever had a tension headache knows just how knotted up the muscles in the back of the neck can get. Periodically stretching this vulnerable area can help ease tension here.

Neck Roll

1. Lift shoulders up by your ears.

2. Rotate the neck and head in large circles three times in each direction.

3. If rotating your head backward hurts your neck, you can instead draw imaginary circles in front of your face with your nose. This provides rotation without the neck tilt.

For Shoulder Tension . . .

When you've been sitting at a computer all day—especially in an uncomfortable chair—the muscles in your middle back can start screaming. Shoulder stretches can release this tension.

Shoulder Stretch

1. Hold your left arm just below the elbow with your right hand.

2. Pull your elbow toward your right shoulder.

3. Hold for three breaths.

4. Repeat on the other side.

Shrugs

Any sort of on-the-job tension can affect the muscles of your shoulders and neck, which can lead to a tension headache. To relax this tension, try this:

1. Rotate your shoulder in a large circle.

2. Push your shoulder blades together, lift the shoulders toward your ears as high as possible.

3. Curl shoulders forward.

4. Pull shoulders toward the floor.

5. Rotate slowly three times in each direction.

Shoulder Release

1. Bring your right arm up over your head.

2. Bend your elbow, placing your right hand on your upper back.

3. Gently pull the right elbow behind your head with your left hand.

4. If you wish, heighten the stretch by pushing the back of your head against your right elbow and lifting your chest.

Chest Expander

1. Lean forward from the hips.

2. Clasp your hands together behind you.

3. Continue to lean forward and inhale while lifting your arms up behind you and lifting and opening your chest.

4. Hold for count of three.

5. Lower arms and take a complete breath.

6. Repeat two times.

Spinal Stretches

All of the muscles in the back can become tense when you're stressed. To relax your spine, lower back and shoulders—and boost oxygen flow to the brain—try the following exercises.

Spinal Exercise #1

1. Place your feet flat on the floor.

2. Lean forward in your chair, relaxing neck, shoulders, and back.

3. Rest your chest on your thighs.

4. Relax your hands toward carpet.

5. Hold for a count of three.

6. Curl your spine as you rise into a sitting position.

Spinal Exercise #2

Some people have a special weakness in the lower back. This exercise is designed to loosen the muscles in this area:

1. Sit up straight, not touching the back of your chair.

2. Cross your legs at the thigh.

3. Put one hand on the outside of the opposite thigh and the other hand on the back of your chair.

4. Look over your shoulder.

5. Sit straight and tall, lifting your chest and pulling shoulders down.

6. Take three deep breaths.

7. Turn forward and repeat on the other side.

Spinal Exercise #3

1. Bend forward and put your right hand along your left foot.

2. Extend your left arm up toward the ceiling and look toward the extended left hand.

3. Hold the position for three deep breaths.

4. Repeat on the other side.

HABITS & STRATEGIES

Stretching active muscles promotes relaxation and helps prevent injuries.

What's Next?

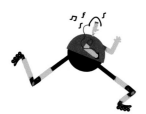

Now you know about proper breathing and stretching. It's time to move on and learn how eating right and jogging off that anxiety can ease your stress.

Diet and Stress

INCLUDES

- Cut out chemical stress
- Nature's tranquilizers
- Mood foods
- Vitamins
- Herbs
- Stress management diet
- Stress-free dieting

FAST FORWARD

Cut Out Chemical Stress ➤ p. 134

Certain foods are the enemies of stress-free living: caffeine, nicotine, alcohol. It's not easy giving up any of them, but relying on a diet laden with these substances can be trouble.

Nature's Tranquilizers ➤ p. 137

Starch and sugar are tranquilizers, initially boosting your energy, only to be followed by a sluggish feeling when insulin cuts the amount of sugar in the blood.

Mood Foods ➤ p. 138

You can influence your mood by what you eat:
- *Calming foods:* Small amounts of carbohydrates
- *Energy-boosters:* Small amounts of protein
- *To get the job done:* Low-fat, protein-rich food
- *Bedtime wind-down:* One to two ounces of warm carbohydrates

Vitamins and Stress ➤ p. 139

Nutritional experts often recommend this antistress vitamin regimen:
- B-complex vitamins
- Vitamins A, C, and E
- Calcium
- Trace elements

Relax with Herbs ➤ *p. 140*

A wide range of herbs can take the edge off a stressful day. Take them as a tea, with fresh or dried leaves:

- Chamomile
- Mint and/or catnip
- American ginseng
- Valerian
- Passionflower

Stress Management Diet ➤ *p. 142*

To manage stress, eat regular, healthy meals. Aim for:

- Fresh fruits and vegetables
- Whole grain bread and grains
- Three meals a day

Stress-Free Dieting ➤ *p. 144*

Occasional lapses are OK when dieting, because the stress of staying on a rigid diet almost guarantees failure.

- Eat with awareness.
- Watch calories, fats, salt, and cholesterol.
- Don't set up rigid dietary restrictions you'll have to endure for a set length of time.
- Make small but consistent changes that you maintain for a lifetime.

Those of you who remember that old computer programmer's maxim of "garbage in, garbage out" already have a head start on this chapter. We're going to focus on the connection between stress and food. Those of you who have ever sat down and demolished an entire carton of Ho-Hos when your life seemed to be falling apart know exactly how comforting some foods can be. Unfortunately, the foods we turn to when we're under stress are usually the ones you won't find on any government food-group chart.

We may not like this fact, but the blunt truth is that to master stress, we have to change. We have to figure out what we're doing that's not healthy and make different lifestyle choices. In this chapter we're going to focus on how stress affects diet—and what a stress management diet might look like. Keep in mind that nutrition is about as controversial as politics or religion. There are countless theories and books out there; the following tips are guidelines that have been digested from a wide variety of sources for you busy people.

Cut Out Chemical Stress

You knew we'd get to it sooner or later—some of the things you like most that seem to help you get through those stressful times can really do some damage.

Cut Out Caffeine

If you're looking for lots of bang for your buck, look no further. Caffeine is a drug—a *stimulant* drug—that actually triggers a stress response in your body.

Caffeine draws the B vitamins out of the body. After the initial perk-up, you'll get an energy drop. If you're really addicted to your morning cup of coffee, your Mallomars for elevenses, or your mug of tea at 4 P.M., you won't want to admit that it can add to stress—but it can.

Moreover, caffeine can add up. While most studies talk about the amount of caffeine in a *cup* of coffee, many people these days drink coffee by the *mug*, not by the cup. When a study says it's probably not going to hurt you to have a cup or two of coffee, that's not the same thing as having two mugs of Java before lunch. There is almost twice as much coffee in a mug as in a cup, and that's twice as much caffeine.

Here's a test:

1. Tomorrow morning, sip on some fruit juice instead of coffee. Then have your regular amount the rest of the day. (Abruptly stopping caffeine can cause nasty headaches.)

2. In a day or so, cut back by another cup.

3. When you start to crave that coffee buzz, try pouring some sparkling water into your mug and sip on that. Keep sipping; most of us don't get enough water anyway.

4. If you really miss the taste of cola drinks and coffee, try drinking caffeine-free cola, a soda that's naturally caffeine-free, or decaf coffee. (There is some residual caffeine in decaf coffee, but not that much.)

5. Cut out chocolate and tea. (No fair reaching for the nonprescription caffeine pills, either!)

You'll want to cut back on caffeine slowly to avoid a headache. That's a withdrawal symptom that happens when your body doesn't get the caffeine jolt it's used to. But after about two weeks, you may start to notice something—you feel different! After three weeks, most people report they feel better with the caffeine out of their systems—they have more energy, and they don't have the swings between energy and inertia.

Here's what you can look forward to:

- Better sleeping
- Calmer nerves

- More energy
- Fewer muscle aches
- Less heartburn
- Fewer headaches (especially if you thought you suffered from sinus headaches)

HABITS & STRATEGIES

If you just can't go caffeine-free cold turkey, try mixing it half-and-half with decaf.

Alcohol in Moderation

In small amounts, a bit of alcohol can help you relax. The problem is that some people can't stop with small amounts. Larger doses of alcohol have the opposite effect. Too much alcohol can actually increase stress because it interferes with healthy, natural sleep.

If you have a problem with drinking, it's most likely adding significantly to your stress in a variety of ways. Seek help from a mental health expert, a 12-step group, or a counselor.

Nicotine

Many people reach for a cigarette, a pipe, or (more recently among baby boomers) a cigar to help them relax. In the very short term, nicotine *does* have that effect on the body. But it doesn't take long before the toxins in smoke raise the heart rate and begin to stress the entire body, from the brain to the immune system. For you doubting Thomases, try this:

- Before you light up that first smoke in the morning, take your pulse.
- Now smoke a cigarette.
- Take your pulse again.

That's your heart on nicotine. It's happening every time you smoke, day in and day out.

Of course, giving up smoking can be a harrowing process that is infinitely more stressful than whatever you were dealing with that made you want to smoke in the first place. But those who have managed to squeak through the awful nicotine withdrawal period report feeling much more relaxed in general than when they smoked.

> ## CAUTION
>
> *Don't eat fat-filled sweets on the assumption that you're helping yourself relax. The fat will slow down the benefits of the sugar, and that high-fat candy bar will end up taking over an hour to help you relax.*

This Diet's No Secret . . .

It turns out your mother was right. Eating a good, well-balanced diet can help you minimize the various types of stress you meet in your daily life.

Starch and Sugar: Nature's Tranquilizers

While people tend to think of sugar as an energy food, in fact it's more of a tranquilizer than anything. It is true that foods rich in sugar can boost your energy over the short haul. But then your body copes with the sugar rush by secreting insulin, which promptly cuts the amount of sugar in the blood. In terms of stress management, sugar gives you a quick burst of energy followed by a low-energy feeling because of the upset balance of the blood sugar level. Some people don't like the feeling, others find it calming. Recent brain-chemistry research has found that both sugar and starch induce relaxation. When you eat these substances, they pave the way for a chemical known as *tryptophan* to enter the brain, where it's converted into the calming chemical known as *serotonin* (the body's own opiate).

If you've had a rough day and you want to relax, try sugar. It works fast— within five minutes—to calm you down. Starches take about 30 minutes.

The following recipes can help you sip away your stress:

1 cup herb tea or decaf coffee

2 tablespoons sugar (not sugar substitute)

Mix together. Sip slowly.

or

1 cup instant cocoa

Water (not milk)

Mix cocoa with hot water. Drink.

HABITS & STRATEGIES

If you'd rather chew your tranquilizers, you don't want to inhale a dozen cream-filled doughnuts under the pretext of getting calm. Do what the French do—nibble just one small roll or two tiny cookies. Try a couple of mints, a lollipop, or some nonfat frozen yogurt.

Hypoglycemics: Stress Attractors

If you suffer from low blood sugar (hypoglycemia) you'll be especially vulnerable to stress, partly because you're feeling tired all the time and partly because hypoglycemia slows down thinking and concentration. If you're already thinking and feeling as if you're made of molasses, you're going to find it that much harder to cope with any stress that comes rolling down the pike.

To control the blood sugar problem, doctors recommend that you eat a high-protein, low-carbohydrate diet broken up into small meals five times a day, with lots of high-protein snacks in between.

CAUTION

There are 8 tablespoons of sugar in one 12-ounce serving of Pepsi or Coca-Cola.

Mood Foods

It's true that we are what we eat. If you want to be grouchy and cranky, then go ahead and eat that junk food. You really can influence your moods by what you eat, and the proper diet can mitigate stress. Specific foods can stimulate or calm.

Calming Foods

Some foods contain an amino acid called *tryptophan,* which stimulates serotonin, a brain chemical that calms you down and can increase concentration. For a natural tranquilizer, eat a small amount of carbohydrates.

Energy-Boosting Foods

Foods containing tryptamine trigger the release of energy-boosting brain chemicals that can give you a boost when your stress levels drag you down. For a natural stimulant, eat a small amount of protein.

Food for a Busy Afternoon

If you need a boost to get those projects finished by the end of the day, choose low-fat, protein-rich foods to increase your motivation, reaction time, and alertness.

Bedtime Wind-Down

To induce a sleepy, relaxed mood, eat a carbohydrate (sweet or starch). Warm food, like tea with honey or sugar or a warm muffin, can provide a sense of nurturing.

CAUTION

Eat no more than 1 to 2 ounces of carbohydrates at bedtime for the desired effect. To avoid piling on pounds, choose a low-fat snack.

Vitamins

Psychological stress—the kind you feel when you're facing a job evaluation—may affect how you process nutrients. If you're stressed out, it's likely you've been running around with an upset stomach tied into knots. Many people under stress don't absorb or digest food as well as they should. Because of this, the vitamin B in your body can become depleted. While you'll certainly want to check with your doctor, nutritional experts often recommend multivitamins and minerals that include the following:

- B-complex vitamins (the antistress vitamins)
- Vitamins A, C, and E
- Calcium
- Trace elements

The Bs are certainly important, you can get them in a healthy diet:

B Vitamin–rich Healthy Diet

- Beans
- Lean meat
- Whole-grain and enriched cereals
- Poultry
- Fish
- Dairy products

If Bs are your target, avoid demineralized cereals, white flour, and white rice.

HABITS & STRATEGIES

Nutritional yeast is an excellent source of B vitamins and can be sprinkled in soups or on salads or added to casseroles.

CAUTION

If you're allergic to wheat, try bread made with corn or some of the sprouted breads that have no wheat in them.

Relax with Herbs

If there's one thing the British understand, it's the restorative properties of a properly brewed "hot cuppa" to take the edge off a stressful day. In fact, herbalists from earliest times have prescribed a variety of herbs brewed in hot water to induce relaxation—recipes that are still in use today.

CAUTION

If you're pregnant or you have health problems, check with your doctor before taking herbs.

If you come home exhausted at the end of the day, reach for one of these teas as a great way to relax. Moreover, most of these come in prepackaged packets you can pick up at any food store chain:

- Chamomile
- Mint
- Catnip
- American ginseng
- Valerian
- Passionflower

Herbalists swear by the relaxing properties of chamomile, which is used around the world by millions of people to lower their stress levels.

Linden–Lemon Balm Tea

3 parts linden flower

2 parts lemon balm

2 parts orange peel

1 part chamomile

1 part lavender

Finely chop the herbs. Rinse the pot with hot water; swish and empty. Then fill with very hot (but not boiling) water. Add 3 teaspoons of herb for each cup of water in the pot; add an extra couple of teaspoons "for the pot." Cover and let steep for 10 minutes.

For those days when you feel tense and stressed with a stomach tied in knots, try this old-fashioned brew. It's guaranteed to help you sleep, calm you down, and ease your stomach.

Mint-Catnip Stomach Soother

Handful of mint leaves (fresh)

Handful of catnip leaves (fresh)

Bruise herbs and place in bottom of pot; cover with very hot water and steep for 10 minutes.

CAUTION

Some people notice an uncomfortable numbing feeling in their throat or tongue from the camphor in the mint and catnip. It's harmless, but it can be startling.

Stress Management Diet

With a little forethought, there are some diet-related ways to minimize stress.

What to Avoid

Being a free spirit may be fun, but when it comes to managing stress you'll do better if your diet is healthy and sensible. Try to avoid the following:

- Bingeing
- Seesaw dieting
- Irregular eating patterns
- Constant overeating

Food to Focus On

If you're battling a stress-filled lifestyle, some of the following tips will help reduce your symptoms. If you're a stress overeater, these ideas should help you drop some pounds, too.

1. Eat more fruits and vegetables. When you're stressed out, your body is crying for calcium—found in green leafy vegetables, which also provide fiber for good elimination.

2. Sure we're busy—and processed food is fast. But the more fresh food you eat, the healthier you'll be. It's easier to grab a piece of fresh fruit from a bowl than to open a can—and much better for you.

3. If your tension tends to manifest itself as indigestion, try eating light meals of fruit or vegetables alone (don't eat them at the same time). If you have trouble digesting all that raw stuff, lightly steam them.

4. For a healthy early-morning breakfast, add a bit of water to apples, bananas, and pears and zap in your microwave for a warm, easy-to-digest breakfast on a cold, sniffly day.

5. Focus on whole-grain bread and grains. Stress robs your body of nutrients (especially the B vitamins).

6. Eat three meals a day—and don't skip breakfast! At the risk of sounding like your mother, it is the most important meal of the day. Stress is made worse by fasting and bingeing.

7. An occasional pan of double-cheese lasagna won't kill you, but follow it by a high-fiber, light meal.

The process of working toward a healthy diet is more important than the goal itself.

How Much Fat Is in There?

The government requires manufacturers to tell you how many grams of fat are in their products, but what you really need to know is the percentage of calories in the food that come from fat. Here's a simple, quick formula to figure it out:

1. *Multiply the grams of fat times 9 to get the calories from fat.*
2. *Divide the calories from fat by total calories (per serving) to get the percentage of fat.*

Example: If whole milk has 8 grams of fat per serving, its calories from fat per serving would be 72. Divide that by 150 (the total calories per serving) and you get 48 percent. This means that 48 percent of the calories in whole milk come from fat.

Stress-Free Dieting

For anyone who's ever abandoned a strict diet after straying into a Boston cream pie, it's important to remember that an occasional dietary lapse is not a serious mistake. Your weekly diet pattern is what's important, not an occasional whoopie pie or fried egg.

When you measure every item that passes your lips, you're treading dangerously close to obsession and high-stress territory. Instead, eat with awareness and watch calories, fats, salt, and cholesterol. A too-rigid diet takes the pleasure out of dining and almost guarantees you'll fail.

- Observe your weekly eating pattern.
- Don't set up restrictions you have to endure for a set time.
- Make tiny but consistent changes toward healthy nutrition within the framework of a lifetime of healthy eating.

What's Next?

Eating well is only half the battle when it comes to handling stress. Getting enough exercise is also important, as you'll learn in the next chapter. Go for it!

CHAPTER

10

Exercise

FAST FORWARD

Get Physical ➤ *p. 148*

The more labor-saving devices our society invents, the less time we spend in physical activity. The result—we're less and less fit to deal with more and more stress. People who lead physically challenging lives have a healthier way of dealing with stress buildup.

Why Fitness Works ➤ *p. 149*

If you're physically fit, you can react better to stress. A regular exercise program offers the following benefits:

1. Lower blood pressure
2. Lower fat in the blood
3. Improved lung capacity
4. Improved cardiovascular system
5. Increase in calming brain wave patterns
6. Decreased muscle tension
7. Improved blood flow to and through the brain

Finding the Time to Exercise ➤ *p. 150*

You need a minimum of two 20-minute exercise sessions per week (three 30-minute workouts are better). You don't need to work as hard as a professional athlete to be physically fit.

Are You Physically Fit? ➤ *p. 151*

Physical fitness means having strong muscles, flexibility, and good heart and lung endurance. To check how you're doing:

1. Subtract your age from 220. That's your maximum heart rate.
2. Multiply that figure by 70 and 85 percent—that's your target heart rate range.
3. When you exercise, check to make sure your heartbeat falls within that range.

Start Sweatin' Away That Stress ➤ *p. 153*

1. Choose an aerobic exercise.
2. Noncompetitive exercise is best.
3. Pick a set time to exercise.
4. Gradually increase exercise intensity and duration.
5. Even a little exercise is better than none.
6. Get an exercise partner.

Top 10 Stress-Busting Exercises ➤ *p. 156*

1. Park farther away from work and walk.
2. Take your pet for longer walks more often.
3. Don't order takeout delivery; walk to the restaurant.
4. Use stairs instead of escalators in stores.
5. Walk on your break, don't nosh.
6. Get off public transportation one stop early and walk.
7. Take the stairs, not the elevator, to your job.
8. Stand instead of sitting.
9. Use a bathroom on another floor.
10. Use a push mower.

You Don't Need Pain to Gain ➤ *p. 160*

If you're in pain after your exercise, even in the beginning, you're doing something wrong. Warm up, cool down, and start slow—you should have little or no muscular discomfort.

You couch potatoes out there might not want to hear this, but experts agree that frequent exercise is probably one of the best stress-reduction techniques there is. You don't have to be an expert, you don't have to exercise every day, and you don't necessarily have to break a sweat—even *walking* can benefit your body. But you do have to grab your sneakers and take that first step. In this chapter, we'll look at the ways exercise can reduce your stress, why it works, and—since we're all busy—which exercises might cut stress the fastest.

Getting Fit in a Technological Society

The age of technology brought us so many nifty labor-saving devices that we're in danger of being the most physically unfit generation ever. Oddly enough, though, all those labor-saving devices haven't protected us from stress. In fact, the more things we can do more quickly, the higher our stress levels seem to rise.

The truth is, every decade we become less and less actively involved in day-to-day activities of survival. When was the last time you fired up a kettle to do your wash? Made your bread from the wheat you plowed yourself? Got your firewood from your own woodlot with your own axe and your own sweat? Consider this:

- You can change the TV channel without raising your head from the sofa pillow.
- You can mow the lawn sitting down.
- You can talk to your cousin in Kuala Lumpur—even see his face if you've got the technology—without ever opening your front door.

There's nothing wrong with labor-saving devices—this book was written on one. But as we become physically insulated from the requirements of survival and our physical activity is mainly in the form of recreation, exercise becomes easier to avoid. Our ancestors didn't have to worry about getting enough exercise, and most of them didn't sit around worrying about whether stress was killing them. But as we become less and less active physically, we also feel less in control of our lives. And that can lead to more stress, too. Getting more exercise can restore not only your response to stress, but your feelings about all aspects of your life. When you feel fit, you feel good about yourself and better able to handle stress.

Why Fitness Works

It's a medical fact that people who are physically fit have a greater capacity to withstand stress than flabby folks who couldn't bench-press a feather pillow. If you're physically toned, you can react less dramatically to physical, mental, and environmental challenges.

According to physiologists, a regular exercise program combats stress in the following ways:

- Lowers blood pressure
- Lowers fat in the blood
- Improves lung capacity
- Increases capillary circulation and blood flow in the arteries
- Conditions the heart

CAUTION

Too much exercise all at once will simply pile on more stress than you need. Start slowly, and gradually increase the length and difficulty of your exercise.

Exercise and Your Brain

You may know that exercise is beneficial for your heart and body and that it helps you handle stress. But did you know that exercise also revs up your brain to boost alertness and help you cope? For example,

- Exercise improves blood flow *to* the brain, toting extra sugar and oxygen along to boost concentration and alertness.
- Exercise speeds blood flow *through* the brain, carrying away the toxic flotsam and jetsam that builds up.
- You can improve this blood flow to the point where even when you're not exercising, waste products are eliminated more efficiently from your brain.
- Exercise increases alpha waves—electrical patterns associated with calmness.
- Exercise raises the endorphin production in your brain.

DEFINITION

endorphins: Substances in the brain related to your mood that give you a feeling of well-being and happiness.

Finding the Time to Exercise

Despite your hectic lifestyle, you should be able to wedge in two 20-minute aerobic workouts each week. Three 30-minute workouts are even better, but the key is to aim for *relaxation,* not to drive yourself crazy trying to fit in an extra exercise session. And no excuses about not having any time. It's a good bet that sometime during the next week, you'll find time to do one or more of the following:

- Watch another episode of Seinfeld.
- Read the obituary section just to see how many people you've survived.
- Water the crabgrass.
- Study the latest Victoria's Secret catalog
- Paint your toenails to match your new outfit.

Exercise can give you the energy you need to cope with unavoidable life stress.

See? We knew you had a few spare 20-minute sessions. Why not exercise instead? One of the reasons that more than 80 percent of adults today aren't active enough to stave off physical deterioration is that most of us assume we have to work as hard as a professional athlete in order to be fit. In fact, you don't need to invest time in a strenuous training program to improve your fitness and deal with stress.

DEFINITION

cardiorespiratory endurance: The ability to perform moderately strenuous large-muscle exercise for relatively long periods of time. If you can walk, bike, jog, or swim for 20 or 30 minutes without falling into a dead swoon, the endurance of your heart and lungs is probably pretty good.

What It Means to Be Physically Fit

There are several indicators of physical fitness:

- Flexibility
- Good muscular function
- Cardiorespiratory endurance

All three of these components are important, but the endurance strength of your heart and lungs is the most important. In order to make sure that you're working your heart and lungs hard enough, of course, you have to have some way of measuring what's going on in there. You can find out by taking your pulse rate.

The average heart is beating along at 72 beats per minute, but there's a lot of variety out there. Generally speaking, the more fit you are the slower your rate will be.

Let's say you choose walking as your exercise workout. A slow meander through the park is nice, but it's of minimal value as an aerobic training exercise. In order to work on your fitness and really reduce your stress, you're going to have to walk fast enough and long enough to get your heart rate up. You can judge how hard your heart is working by measuring how fast your heart beats during workouts. In order to do this, you'll need to do two things:

1. Determine your *maximum heart rate*.

2. Calculate your *target heart rate range*.

Finding Your Maximum Heart Rate

Your maximum heart rate is a lot like the top speed of your car. Your manual *says* your new Toyota will go 110 mph, but you wouldn't want to spend your life driving that fast. Likewise, your maximum heart rate is the maximum it should ever be, not the rate your heart *should* be working when you exercise.

You don't need to be Stephen Hawking to figure out your maximum heart rate. Just subtract your age from 220. If you're 40, here's what you do:

$$\begin{array}{r} 220 \\ -40 \\ \hline \end{array}$$

Maximum heart rate: 180 beats per minute

Your Target Heart Rate Range

Next you'll want to figure out your target heart rate range—this is the heartbeat that you're aiming for when you exercise. The target heart rate range is 70 to 85 percent of the maximum heart rate. Again, assume you are 40:

1. Take your maximum heart rate (180 beats per minute)
2. Multiply .70 times 180 (126 beats per minute)
3. Multiply .85 times 180 (153 beats per minute)

When you exercise, you'd want your pulse to be somewhere between 126 and 153 beats per minute the whole time. It's a good idea to start out exercising lightly so that your heart rate stays in the lower part of your heart rate range. This way, you'll be able to keep going for the full 20 or 30 minutes. If you've been pretty much of a sloth in the past, you'll be surprised at how little exercise it takes to get your heart beating faster.

As you become more experienced, you can turn up the heat and do more strenuous exercising, which will boost your heart rate into the higher ranges.

HABITS & STRATEGIES

To make things easier, convert your one-minute heart rates into 10-second rates so you have to take your pulse for only 10 seconds. To convert, simply divide your target rates by 6. A 40-year-old would have a target 10-second range of between 21 and 25 beats.

Most people mistakenly believe that exercise will boost their appetite. In fact, most sedentary people eat more calories than active folks.

Four Spots to Take Your Pulse

1. *Carotid artery:* This may be the easiest spot to feel your pulse. Place your fingers between your Adam's apple and the large muscles of your neck. You may need to slide your fingers around to find the best spot.

2. *Wrist:* Place your first two fingers (*not* your thumb) lightly on the underside of your wrist, right below the thumb.

3. *Temple:* Place two fingers lightly at either temple.

4. *Over your heart:* Place your hand over the left side of your body just below the breast.

Sweatin' Away the Stress

OK, you've decided to give exercise a try. Here are a few tips to keep you heading in the right direction:

1. Pick an activity that is *aerobic.* This might include walking, running, cross-country skiing, tennis, swimming. Whatever you choose, select something you enjoy doing; you'll be more likely to stick with it that way.

2. Pick a set time to exercise. If you have back-to-back meetings most afternoons and lots of dinner business engagements, then select an early-morning exercise time—a time you're likely to be regularly available.

3. You may be a whiz on the tennis court, but keep in mind that non-competitive exercise is usually less stressful. You're exercising for enjoyment, not for a chance to grind your opponent into the dust.

4. Try to exercise three times a week for 20 minutes, and then gradually increase both intensity and duration.

5. Remember, a little exercise is still better than none. If you can't commit to a three-day-a-week exercise schedule, don't give up on the idea of exercise completely.

6. If you're having trouble keeping up with your exercise, think about getting an exercise partner. Exercising can reduce stress, and so can

social interaction. Combining the two can really boost your relaxation efforts.

Aerobics Is Important

Aerobic exercise isn't limited to a group class where everyone wears coordinated outfits and steps their way to fitness. If you dribble a basketball, ride a bike, jog around a track, play racquetball, ice-skate, water-ski, jump rope, swim laps, play tennis, or dance the Funky Chicken, you are engaging in aerobic exercise. If you're using oxygen to produce energy, that's all it takes.

DEFINITIONS

Aerobic: Any exercise that creates a demand for oxygen, involves large-muscle groups and gets your heart rate up.
Anaerobic: Exercises that require less oxygen (such as weight lifting) and that don't provide overall health benefits to heart and lungs.

Any Exercise Is Good

Aerobic exercises come in two styles—*continuous* (walking or running) and *intermittent* (tennis or walk-jog programs). If you're just sticking a toe into this exercise business and you're less than fit, you probably should start with an intermittent activity. You can then work up to an intermittent program once you become healthier, since you'll get the most results from a low-intensity, continuous workout.

The following are Continuous exercises:

- Brisk walking
- Swimming
- Riding your bike
- Dancing
- Mowing the lawn

Here's a sampling of Intermittent exercises

- Tennis
- Working in the garden
- Jog-walk programs

Warm Up, Cool Down

Busy people like shortcuts. But shortcuts aren't *always* the answer. If we don't copy our computer disks, we'll go nuts when our hard drive turns to stone. If we don't floss twice a day we may have to sit in the dentist's office for three hours having a root canal. If we don't warm up and cool down, we may wonder what we're doing in the cardiac care section of the hospital.

There are good shortcuts and there are harmful shortcuts. An ill-considered shortcut ends up costing us *lots* of time. In the case of warm-ups and cooldowns, not doing them can have unfortunate physical consequences.

Warm-Up Period

You wouldn't jump in your old car on a frigid day and stomp on the gas, would you? Just as idling the car allows engine parts to be lubricated for smooth running, light stretching before exercise can limber and warm the muscles you're going to be using during your workout. If you spend 30 minutes exercising, you need to add on about 8 minutes of warm-up first (longer for beginners). Light stretches should include the following:

- Lower-back stretch
- Hamstring stretch
- Calf-muscle stretch

Then you begin a slow rehearsal of the aerobic exercise to raise your metabolic rate to your target rate.

Cooldown Period

There's nothing wrong with slamming on the brakes of your Buick and stopping whenever you want, but your body is a lot more sensitive than an old Buick. As you've been exercising, the blood vessels in your legs have expanded to speed up the flow of blood. As your leg muscles contract, it helps push the blood through the veins and back to the heart. When you stop, blood tends to pool in

Warm-Up Stretches

Do these light stretches for only one or two counts. Repeat three times for each leg.

Calf Stretch

1. *Put your right foot in a straight line behind your left foot.*
2. *Bend your left leg until the knee is over your toe.*
3. *Keep your right leg straight and your right heel on the ground.*
4. *Switch legs and repeat.*

Hamstring Stretch

1. *Put right foot on something lower than your hips.*
2. *Lean forward a little from the chest, with your chin up.*
3. *Switch legs and repeat.*

your legs instead of being pumped back to your heart, which is still beating at exercise target rate. As a result, the volume of blood reaching the heart drops suddenly, threatening the brain. You may feel faint. And because the coronary arteries may not get enough blood, the heart may begin beating irregularly. Heart attack can follow.

When Exercise Is Too Intense

We are all busy people, and the tendency for busy people is to push too hard too fast. It doesn't work well when it comes to exercise. If you exercise too hard when you first start, you're more likely to hurt yourself. And if you're doing something that boosts your heart rate beyond your target range, you're forcing your body to turn to internal sources of energy. This doesn't bode well for those of you who are trying to lose weight by exercising. As the body burns sugar stored in muscle instead of fat calories, your rate of weight loss drops.

Some of you out there are likely still dragging your heels. It is a busy world, and maybe between your job, your friends and family, your home, and your volunteer activities, you just don't think you can work in extra time for exercise.

You don't get excused for lack of time. Instead, figure out ways to incorporate exercise into your daily life.

If you can't carry on a conversation with the person next to you while you're working out, you are exercising too hard.

Cooldown Stretches

Hold each of these stretches without bouncing. Gently lean into the stretch until you feel light tension. Breathe and relax. After the tension has eased, lean farther, until you reestablish a light tension. Breathe and relax again until the tension subsides. Hold from 10 to 20 seconds. Repeat all these stretches four times for each leg.

Calf Stretch

1. *Put your right foot in a straight line behind your left foot.*
2. *Bend your left leg until the knee is over your toe.*
3. *Keep your right leg straight and your right heel on the ground.*
4. *Switch legs and repeat.*

Knee Hug

1. *Lie on your back with knees slightly bent.*
2. *Gently hug one knee to your chest by reaching under your upper leg.*
3. *Pull your leg closer to your body to increase stretch.*
4. *Switch legs and repeat.*

Hamstring Stretch

1. *Lie on your back with both knees bent.*
2. *Gently hug one knee to your chest by reaching under your upper leg.*
3. *Slowly straighten your leg until you feel a light tension.*
4. *Straighten your leg more to feel more stretch.*
5. *Switch legs and repeat.*

Quad Stretch

1. *Stand on your left leg.*
2. *Reach behind with your left hand and grab your right foot.*
3. *Press your foot against your buttocks with your hand until you feel light tension in your thigh.*
4. *Switch legs and repeat.*

Top 10 Stress-Busting Exercises

Are you having fun exercising, or are you just substituting one type of stress for another? If you don't like your workout, it's going to be hard to stick with it.

1. Park in the garage two blocks from your office instead of in the lot next door. Walk every day to and fro.

2. If you have a pet, snap on that leash and go one block farther than usual, faster than usual. Then add another block. Or try walking more often.

3. Hankering for an order of mu shu pork? Put down the phone and walk to the restaurant.

4. On your way to the bargain basement, take the stairs instead of the escalator.

5. Just before they wheel the pastry cart past your desk, take your break by walking outside, wandering over to your buddy's cubicle, or dropping by Employee Benefits to check up on your pension. (With all this exercise, chances are you'll be around to collect!)

6. If you take the subway or bus, get off one stop earlier and walk the rest of the way.

7. Try taking the stairs to and from your office every day. But do this gradually—especially if you work on the 39th floor. Try to add one flight each week.

8. At the next cocktail party, try standing and chatting instead of sitting down beside the tortilla chip bowl.

9. Use the bathroom on the floor below or above yours.

10. Don't use a riding lawn mower when you can push one. You might even consider using an old-fashioned push mower (the kind without a motor).

Easing the Fight-or-Flight Rush

Taking a 30-minute jog around the parking lot is also another good way to wind down after a heart-stopping, adrenaline-pumping incident (like a fight with your partner). Remember that prehistoric ancestor arm-wrestling the woolly mammoth in Chapter 1? Adversity can trigger a fight-or-flight response that sends a jolt of energy surging through your body—whether you need it or not. After a stress-filled event, those circulating stress hormones are still spinning around in there. Exercise can burn off the adrenaline released during a fight-or-flight response the way it was meant to be burned off, according to Herbert Benson, M.D., president of the Mind/Body Medical Institute of Harvard's Deaconess Hospital in Boston.

CAUTION

There are a lot of wrong approaches to exercise that could damage your body over the long run. After you read this book, you might want to find a reputable, up-to-date expert to help you devise a customized exercise plan just for you.

Baseball Glove or Jai Alai Mitt? You Decide!

Exercise, after all, is exercise. You can reduce stress whether you simply choose to walk down the block to Baskin-Robbins or slam a racquetball around with your old college buddies. Do whatever works. As the folks at Nike say, *just do it.*

For some people, the idea of being shut inside a paneled room with a ball as hard as a walnut and an opponent intent on annihilation is far more stressful than anything they might encounter in the job world. Others find all that crashing and smashing to be relaxing.

Choose exercise that you enjoy doing and that you're likely to stick with. The goal is to release your stress through healthy exercise, not to create more of it by doing something that makes you uncomfortable.

Take Your Vitamins

In addition to all those other benefits, regular exercise apparently boosts the ability of vitamins C and E in their efforts to improve immune function. In one study, subjects who exercised had more infection-fighting cells whether or not they also took vitamins.

Clear Your Mind

When you've got so many projects and hassles competing for your attention, it's hard to keep them all straight. Many people report one of the main components of stress is feeling overwhelmed. It's hard to concentrate on the work in front of you when 10 other situations are screaming for your attention at the same time.

When this happens to you, it's time to get up from your desk and do something *physical.* If you have the time, go work out at your athletic club. Go swimming. Or just take a brief walk. If your office building has stairs, don't wait for a fire drill. Take a quick walk down to the lobby and back up as a way of clearing the cobwebs out of your mind. When you get back to your desk, you'll be better able to cope with the stress of all those projects.

CAUTION

If you're over 35 or in poor physical condition, don't start an exercise program before you see a doctor for a physical exam and a treadmill test.

You Don't Need Pain to Gain!

If you're a typical weekend exerciser, you probably have vivid memories of beginning some sport or exercise and walking around in agony for the next week or so from protesting muscles. The truth is, if you're in pain after you start to exercise, you're probably exercising incorrectly.

If you warm up and cool down, you should have little or no pain. If you're hobbling around the next day and your muscles are screaming so loudly your teeth hurt, you can take that as a signal you've done too much. *Stiff, sore muscles are not a sign that you're getting stronger. They're a sign that you were too busy to warm up and cool down properly.*

You burn almost the same number of calories whether you walk or jog.

Exercise-related Warning Signs

You need to be aware of potential problems while exercising, especially if you're just starting after years of inactivity. Any of the following signs are warnings to stop exercising and see your doctor:

- *Excessive tiredness*
- *Unusual joint, muscle, or ligament problems*
- *Chest pain*
- *Pain in teeth, jaws, or ears*
- *Light-headedness, dizziness, or fainting*
- *Nausea or vomiting*
- *Headache*
- *Shortness of breath*
- *Sustained increase in heart rate after slowing down or resting*
- *Irregular pulse*

What's Next?

This is where our discussion of stress draws to a close, but *your* efforts are just beginning. For more information about lots of interesting stress-related topics, check out the appendixes. Good luck!

11

Wrapping Up

FAST FORWARD

Setting Your Goals ➤ *p. 166*

It takes time to learn how to control stress. You may have to unlearn some behaviors, readjust your focus, and be disciplined enough to pay attention to your new goals.

What Really Matters? ➤ *p. 167*

It's not easy to de-stress your life. Take a few minutes to consider the following:

- When was the last time you sat on the floor with your kids and played what they wanted?
- When was the last time you were spontaneous?
- When was the last time you noticed your surroundings?
- Are you on autopilot more and more these days?

Stress Management Goal-Setting Plan ➤ *p. 168*

It's essential to plan how to control your stress. Goal setting is a good way to do this.

1. Put your goals in writing.
2. Make your goals tough but attainable.
3. Set short-term goals.
4. Create goals in all aspects of your life.
5. Don't forget long-term goals.
6. Vividly imagine accomplishing your goal.
7. Pick goals you really desire.
8. Take steps to reach those goals.
9. Make a commitment.
10. Plan new goals each New Year or on each birthday.

Practice, Practice, Practice \blacktriangleright p. 169

Changing your patterns of exercise, diet, relaxation, and time management all take practice and commitment—and time. But it's doable.

Taking Control \blacktriangleright p. 170

If you're going to make your life less stressful, the responsibility is yours. You have to take control. It's not easy, but many have already taken these steps and succeeded. You can, too.

Well, here we are. Despite your busy schedule, you've made it to the last chapter of the book. Here you'll learn how to pull it all together—how to move ahead to reach your goals while keeping stress in check. This isn't really the end—it's a beginning.

Setting Your Goals

The U.S. Public Health Service has made reducing stress by the year 2000 one of its major health-promotion goals.

Rome wasn't built in a day, and it's not likely that you're going to reach your stress management goals in 24 hours, either. It has taken you most of your life to get to the point where you are now stresswise. To undo all that damage, you may have to unlearn some behaviors, readjust your focus, and be disciplined enough to pay attention to your new goals.

The Rewards Are Worth It

When you're looking at lifestyle changes and long-term behavior modification, sometimes the process seems a bit daunting. Your high-stress life may not bother you unless you're in the middle of a tension explosion. It may be hard to find the motivation to de-stress if you haven't had a heart attack, gotten to divorce court, or punched out an annoying salesperson. Some people genuinely like living in the midst of hurricanes. They feel alive with papers flying in all directions, someone barking orders, and deadlines looming.

HABITS & STRATEGIES

Sometimes it's OK simply to do nothing. Schedule at least 15 minutes every day simply to do nothing.

Avoid making promises you can't keep.

Long-Term Costs

Odds are that you'll pay a very high price for getting to work a few minutes sooner, taking on more projects to earn a few extra dollars, or being able to juggle six balls and a frying pan at the same time. Today, the price you pay is having less time to do the things that really matter.

Ultimately, the price you pay may be your life.

What Really Matters?

Most people who are caught up in frantic, stress-filled busyness are so intent on looking down the road to prepare for the next crisis that they often overlook the gifts right at their feet.

As you make the final decision to commit to a stress management plan, take a few minutes to consider the following:

- When was the last time you let your kids direct on-the-floor play ("I'll be the Incredible Slam Man, Dad, and you be the horrible scaggy alien from the Planet Blecch") instead of acting as general contractor for Lincoln Logs, Inc.?
- When was the last time you spontaneously ditched your Saturday plans to pick out a new circular saw and took your kids to see *Hercules* instead—just because they asked?
- When was the last time you noticed the color of the sky at dusk, the scent of wood smoke on the wind, or the way your daughter's nose scrunches up when she's studying?
- Have you caught yourself getting to work without any memory of the trip you took to get there?
- Are you on autopilot more and more these days?
- Do you find yourself riding elevators or carousels? Do you pick administrative assistants or daisies? Smell copier fluid or new-mown hay?

No one on his or her deathbed ever regretted not spending more time in the office.

Yes, yes, we hear you. Life is a serious business, not a theme park. We're all adults here—busy adults—and we've got responsibilities and duties and jobs. But coming to terms with modern-day stress means that sometimes it's OK to put down the burden. Sometimes it's OK to laugh.

In fact, you'll be healthier and happier if you do.

STRATEGIES & HABITS

Learn to say no. You'll be facing many requests for your time—phone conversations, unscheduled or extended meetings, social invitations. Ask yourself: Do I really want or need to go along?

Stress Management Goal-Setting Plan

You can keep your eye out for a little relaxing fun and still be serious about life. One of the best ways to avoid stress and have more time for other important things is to sit down and develop a plan for handling your stress.

1. We all need goals. Get some. Put them in writing so you know you'll be serious about them.

2. If you don't have a written goal, it's not really a goal, it's just a wish. You won't usually take wishes as seriously as goals.

3. When you're writing your goal, it shouldn't be so lofty that it can't be attained. But it shouldn't be so easy that it doesn't take work. Aim for a goal that's better than your current best, but not so high that the stress of trying to reach it will cause you to get frustrated and give up.

4. Set short-term goals. Reaching a goal is rewarding. If you don't build in positive reinforcement, you may get discouraged before you get to your long-term goals.

5. Don't limit goals to the area of stress management. Setting goals will help you handle stress, but aim for goals in all aspects of your life: family, health, recreation, spiritual growth. If all your goals involve work, you're pushing yourself right back into that stress loop.

6. Don't forget long-term goals. Who do you want to be? Where do you want to go? And, that perennial favorite job-interview question, where do you want to be in five years?

If you can identify your priorities, decision making and goal setting become much easier.

7. Vividly imagine accomplishing your goal. Use your imagery and visualization techniques from Chapter 7. Rehearse the goals.

8. It's not enough to think that you "sort of want to travel to Bora Bora." You must vividly, passionately *yearn* to go to Bora Bora. If you don't really care, you'll never make it.

9. Take steps to reach that goal. Don't read *Popular Mechanics* if you want to visit Bora Bora; start reading *Travel & Leisure*.

10. Make a commitment: "I want to be the best vice president in the company in 24 months." "I want to drive a Ferrari Testarossa by my high school reunion next year."

11. Some people make a new goal for themselves at each New Year or on each birthday.

Practice, Practice, Practice

As long as you keep practicing the techniques to de-stress your life, you will accomplish what you are working for.

Exercise, healthy diet, relaxation, time management—all these skills take practice. You won't be able to automatically transform your life just by reading a page or two from this or any other book.

Change takes work and commitment. But you know you have those skills—that's probably what brought you to the stress-filled life you've got now!

Change Takes Time

Integrating these techniques so they feel automatic may take some time. Busy people never like to hear that. But once you succeed in changing your diet or doing more exercises it becomes easy. You should be able to make incremental changes without disrupting your life. And most of the changes won't add time to your busy days. It just may take a while until you incorporate the changes without thinking about them.

Constant Instant Practice

As you go about integrating all of your stress management techniques, think about "constant instant practice." Every hour, take a few moments to relax. This can help break your stress cycle and help you get into the habit of managing stress.

As you practice some of the instant relaxing techniques we discussed earlier, think about how you're feeling at the moment. This will help remind you of the stress you're meeting every day. Only when you are aware of this stress in your life can you hope to change it.

Taking Control

It's usually your interpretation of a situation that you find stressful, not the situation itself. You aren't afraid to walk across a board resting on the ground, but walking across a board 6 feet off the ground is scary because you are imagining what might happen.

Your ability to highlight the areas of stress in your life and set about making changes is fundamentally about taking control of your own life. Nobody else is going to wake you up in the morning and hand you your running shoes. Your boss isn't going to stick her head in your door and whisper, "It's time to do those neck rolls now!"

It's all about changing your own point of view. About taking control of your own health, your own life, and your own happiness. If you value yourself, you'll find ways to build your new outlook into your life.

It can be hard to start. One reason more people may not start de-stressing their lives is that it looks hard. You may have to give up Big Macs and Milky Ways for breakfast. Exercising takes some motivation.

But people who have gone before you—and many have taken the steps necessary to de-stress their lives—say that when you succeed, you don't miss your old, unhealthy, slothful ways. As stress falls away, true balance takes it place.

HABITS & STRATEGIES

Everyday fears add stress for lots of people. If this is your problem, write down your fears, note similarities, and rank them. Little by little, expose yourself to those things that scare you.

A

Handy Stress-Related Web Sites

Center of Anxiety and Stress

This website includes an anxiety-symptom checklist, advice on counseling, and information on the book *Overcoming Panic Attacks.*

http://www.cts.com/~health

Health and Fitness Journals

This fee-based service from CompuServe offers a list of pertinent articles about a variety of any topics. Just type in a subject of interest.

COMPUSERVE: *go* **HLTDB**

Mental Health Com

Free encyclopedia of mental health.

http://www.mentalhelh.comp1.html

Mental Health Net

Search "stress" for related articles.

http:/cmhc.com/

No-Nonsense Stress Cures That Really Work

A Web site filled with helpful information.

http://www.stresscure.com/

Stress and Anxiety Research Society

Web site for a professional group dedicated to stress.

http://www.uib.no/STAR

Stress Busters

A Web site listing a variety of stress-busting techniques.

http://www.stressrelease.com/strssbs.html

Stress-free Net

A handy Web site with information about therapists' referrals, "ask the psychologists," and tests.

http://stressfree.com/

Mailing lists
ANXIETY-L
Subscribers to this active list share their feelings about anxiety.

Stress and Coping Test

The following situations are often found to be stressful. Check off any that you think might apply to you over the next year, and indicate your coping level for each.

Coping Levels

1. **Burned out:** Severe difficulty in coping, profound feelings of anxiety, dread, depression, helplessness, and/or anger that interferes with job or personal life. Presence of physical symptoms, such as lowered immunity, tension, depleted energy.

2. **Strained:** Frequent problems with coping; sense of being overwhelmed or drained; persistent feelings of anxiety, anger, irritability, helplessness, and/or worry with accompanying problems at work or home.

3. **Balanced:** Effective, stable functioning at work and home with only occasional uncomfortable yet appropriate feelings.

4. **Highly effective:** Extremely effective. Feeling challenged, energized, motivated, and successful.

Job Pressures

1. I feel as if I have too many responsibilities and deadlines.
___ Stressed out
___ Strained
___ Balanced
___ Highly effective

2. I always end up disagreeing with customers, co-workers, superiors, or management.
___ Stressed out
___ Strained
___ Balanced
___ Highly effective

3. I feel a lack of control over my job responsibilities.
   __ Stressed out
   __ Strained
   __ Balanced
   __ Highly effective

4. My job is subject to layoffs, downsizing, reorganizations, and cut-backs.
   __ Stressed out
   __ Strained
   __ Balanced
   __ Highly effective

5. There's not much opportunity for advancement.
   __ Stressed out
   __ Strained
   __ Balanced
   __ Highly effective

6. I have too much (or too little) contact with people.
   __ Stressed out
   __ Strained
   __ Balanced
   __ Highly effective

7. I have too many hassles and interruptions on my job.
   __ Stressed out
   __ Strained
   __ Balanced
   __ Highly effective

Personal Issues

8. I've experienced the death of a significant person in my life this past year.
   __ Stressed out
   __ Strained
   __ Balanced
   __ Highly effective

9. I'm separated or divorced.
   ___ Stressed out
   ___ Strained
   ___ Balanced
   ___ Highly effective

10. I've had a serious illness or injury.
    ___ Stressed out
    ___ Strained
    ___ Balanced
    ___ Highly effective

11. I'm in financial trouble.
    ___ Stressed out
    ___ Strained
    ___ Balanced
    ___ Highly effective

12. I've had conflicts with my partner, in-laws, family, and friends.
    ___ Stressed out
    ___ Strained
    ___ Balanced
    ___ Highly effective

13. I have sexual conflicts and/or frustration.
    ___ Stressed out
    ___ Strained
    ___ Balanced
    ___ Highly effective

14. I have problems with my children.
    ___ Stressed out
    ___ Strained
    ___ Balanced
    ___ Highly effective

15. I have spiritual or religious conflicts.
    ___ Stressed out
    ___ Strained